UPLEVEL YOUR LIFE

The Unapologetic Guide to Manifesting Success

Toni Moore, Esq.

PUBLISHING SERVICE BY: Pen Legacy®
COVER & EDITING BY: Five-Fold Media Publishing, Rita T. Henderson
FORMATTING BY: U Can Mark My Word, Carla M. Dean

ISBN # 978-1-7364112-9-2

DEDICATION

*To all the women
who crave to live their dreams,
don't settle...Uplevel.*

UPLEVEL YOUR LIFE

The Unapologetic Guide to Manifesting Success

Prelude

I recall a few years back waiting for a valet to return my luxury vehicle so I could get into my very comfortable bed in my suburban dream home. While driving from the event, I heard on the radio that the traffic on 76 West was bumper to bumper, so I quickly rerouted towards Broad Street. As I sped the sports vehicle through the traffic lights, I noticed some of my old stomping grounds from my college and graduate school years now included a grocery store, movie theatre, stores, and a few other commercial entities that now rivaled the surroundings of my alma mater in West Philly, the University of Pennsylvania. While sitting impatiently at a stoplight near Temple University's campus, I was surprised to see a young woman walking up Broad Street alone. Back in my college days, young women traveled in packs. I almost jumped out of my seat when I heard an older man's voice call out to the girl from a newer model Mercedes Benz. I let the light turn from green to yellow and then red while prayerfully willing the young lady not to prance towards the vehicle. As she tiptoed towards the car in a short skirt that skimmed her thick thighs, I prayed she would refuse an invitation to sit in the car's buttery leather seat. But I knew she wouldn't because I didn't many years ago.

I didn't care whether or not she was a student at Temple University. I just didn't want her to fall victim to those who preyed on girls who prayed for love. With bated breath, I watched the scene unfold as the young lady stayed a little too long talking at the window. But I said nothing and did nothing despite wanting to do something. I thought about rolling down the window and telling her to move on, but I didn't. I thought about interrupting the conversation as someone had tried to do a few times for me when I was in college, but I didn't. I even thought about pulling over to the side to offer her a ride, but I didn't. Instead, I watched for a little while longer until an irate driver awakened me from my stupor, and I proceeded up Broad Street towards home.

For whatever reason, I couldn't shake the feeling that I could have done something to possibly change the trajectory of the girl's destiny. I wondered what I should have or could have done for that young lady or what I would have done if she was my niece. As the early morning became night, the conviction subsided. But seemingly, God had other plans since after seeing the young woman, I began noticing other young girls, ladies, and women who were living as though they had no choice about their outcome. Somehow, the women I saw reminded me of my younger self, who wanted so badly to live happily ever after. I stumbled, fell, got up, and tried again and again. But, if not for the help from others, I don't know where I would be. Eventually, God got my attention when He asked me in His own special way whether I could live with the outcome if women who I was called to serve failed to become whom He created them to be. That got my attention!

Acknowledgments

To my husband and biggest supporter in our business, thank you for helping me appreciate that I could live my "happily ever after" from anywhere in the world.

To Momma Cint, who has always been a superstar, trailblazing Diva Extraordinaire who lives her best life.

To my boys, thank you for helping me appreciate that every generation gets an opportunity to make tomorrow better.

To my pastor and spiritual mentors, thank you for being a living, walking, and talking miracle that continually inspires me.

To my writing coach, who has been an integral part of my business's growth, thank you for awakening me to my possibilities.

And to all my sisters, cousins, and/or girlfriends, one more book done and many more to go—Lord willing.

Introduction

If you don't like what is happening or what could happen, you have the power to say "This is not how my story will end."

— Unknown

When Momma was almost eighteen years old, she committed the cardinal sin of getting pregnant outside of matrimony. As a result, Momma was removed from singing in the choir and other church activities. My momma was stubborn about disclosing the name of my sister's father. She tried to avoid the church walk of shame that was forced upon women by saying my father had impregnated her. But my father realized her lie when my sister started looking like one of the two preaching brothers when she was about five months. Unfortunately, everyone knew Momma because she was an amazing singer. They also knew her because she was an embarrassment to her father, who was not only a preacher but a proud military veteran who once served as a Master Sergeant in the United States Army. Momma was forced to leave school because that's what happened when teen girls got pregnant. On top of that, Momma lost custody of her daughter and was sent to live with another family member in a different state.

As Momma took the perp walk of shame, no one noticed how she angrily looked at the young aspiring preacher who impregnated her. He didn't even know he was the father because Momma never told him until my sister was almost thirteen. Nor did anyone see Momma's loving gaze upon her young lover—the pastor's grandson who served as the church's bass player. Momma did what she had to do to return to the only thing that brought joy to her life—singing. Almost two years after Momma shared her heartfelt promise of celibacy before the entire congregation, she gave birth to me.

But true to Momma's word, she never partook in the Christian girl's walk of shame again because, within days of my birth, Granddaddy forced a sweet southern man to be my daddy. I didn't know the person Momma and Grandmom pretended to be my dad wasn't really my dad when I laid eyes on him. He was the most stable person I knew until I was snatched away from him when I was almost four years old. I didn't see him again until I was eleven. And after we reconnected, we had a disjointed relationship until I met the man who bore my cheeks, nose, and complexion right before my 39th birthday. Prior to meeting my father, I had met and lived with two men whom Momma told me were my daddy. I was too old to go through the birth story yet again. So, I asked him how did he know I was his. During our fateful forty-minute conversation,

I listened to my father speak about his last kiss with my momma. I imagined a different side of Momma that I got glimpses of. Momma—young, happy, in love, and full of hope. Someone I got a chance to see every once in a while.

I took a picture with him and sent it to my daddy. I'm such an advocate for the truth that I reached out to my dad to tell him what I had learned. Daddy told me that the devil was always busy. So, I sent him a picture that spoke volumes. At first, he didn't give me a response. But, after asking for forgiveness for being a part of a ruse that I never knew I was a co-conspirator of, Daddy shared with me a story of a little girl who was snatched from him. After my parents divorced within three years of meeting, a family court judge gave my daddy custody. But living with Daddy was short-lived because my mother and her new husband came and snatched me up within a year of the custody court order. Daddy told me that I reached out to him at four years old through my babysitter, but he never came to get me. More than thirty-five years after Daddy failed to rescue me, I asked him if he still wanted to be my daddy. I didn't pressure him, nor did I beg him to stay. So, when he stopped calling to check on my sons and me, I respected his decision.

When I learned about my biological father's death, I was hesitant. I didn't know whether to trek to Harrisburg to sit amongst strangers or stay home amongst the family I gave birth to. As I hesitated to and fro, I recalled several short telephone calls with my father wherein he confided that he also was raised as another man's child. Unfortunately, he never got a chance to meet his father because when he and his family went to meet him, they learned my grandfather had died. My father never met his father nor his family since he turned around after learning of his passing. I didn't want to be like my father. So, I decided to go to my father's funeral.

As I took the drive on the Pennsylvania Turnpike, I imagined a reception wherein I would finally meet the relatives my heart knew but my eyes had never seen. As I walked down the same aisle that Momma walked down, I ignored the fact that I was heading towards where my momma could never sit—the front row. As I took in the irony of sitting up front, I looked to see who was in the audience. Much to my shock, my older sister's father was presiding over my father's funeral. I sat and tried to pretend that I always knew what others did. I mean, not too many people would know the difference since I moved from my small town with big secrets when I graduated from Milton Hershey School. I would be beckoned home on a few occasions or visit for weddings and funerals. But my childhood trauma and familial triggers kept me from showing up regularly.

As the pastor spoke, I nodded. When my siblings shared their life experiences, I nodded. Even when I heard how great my father was, I nodded. But when the family videos were shared, I had to leave. All of my life, I had wished my real daddy would show up and save me from my life experiences and circumstances, but he never did. While I never knew my daddies were my biological fathers, I lived through rejection, abandonment, hurt, and pain. In the midst of my dark experience, no one came to save me. It was too much for me to take in at once. So, I bolted from the front row to the bathroom. I had to release the scream in my spirit without making a sound. I had come too far to lose my mind at a stranger's funeral—a man who I met for less than sixty minutes in a parking lot.

While I walked back with my head up, freshly fixed face, and newly applied lipstick, I told myself to boss up. Despite living within the gutters of Harrisburg, I built myself by refusing to be the person everyone talked about. To keep the tears from rolling from my eyes, I imagined having a dramatic showdown with my older sister's father. When the funeral ended, my siblings asked me to hang out at the repass to meet other family members. While I agreed to put on my big girl panties and red lipstick, I needed to meet with one of my mother's baby's daddies.

I didn't show up as the weepy, scarred, and scared little girl who he knew me to be when he came through time and time again throughout my childhood. I showed up like the lawyer I became—ready, willing, and able to exorcise the secrets from his soul. I needed to know why he never said anything once I was good and grown. I wanted to know why he never reached out to me through my older sister. After all, he knew my number to inquire about legal issues regarding his personal life and automotive business. I had questions, and since my mother and my father were both gone, I went to the one person who was unknowingly part of my mother's love triangle. Pastor or not, I was ready to give him a piece of my mind. After all, he knew me for almost twenty years of my life. He laughed with Momma, reminisced as only good friends could, and shared secrets with her, too. I needed to know how this man—who smiled in my face, wined and dined with my momma, and pretended to care about my well-being—kept such a big secret from me. However, the only thing he did when I asked him why he never felt I was worthy of knowing who fathered me was smirk and tell me it was my mother's business.

I felt like pimp slapping him and all of the other people who gossiped with friends and family about how I ran out of the funeral because I was emotionally distraught. I mean, I was sitting in the front row of the same church that my momma had attended. I was sitting with siblings whom I never knew existed but who shared some of my DNA. And I was the center of an almost forty-year-old secret that everyone knew, but no one was sympathetic enough to tell me. As I looked around at all of the familiar faces, I thought of my momma walking down the perp walk of shame to try to convince the church pastors and elders that she was a sinner with a contrite heart. I imagined Momma taking the perp walk of shame to confess her sins so she could sing the solo part of the hymnals. I'm sure her choir was much like a sorority that helped her belong. So much so that she found a great man to pretend to be my father.

The only thing I could do was look at him as though he could feel my stern glare. By the time my father had passed away, I had built a reputation and career that was worthy of protection. I couldn't stoop so low to relegate to the person I used to be. I didn't allow myself to plead or cry before him. Instead, I walked away with tears in my eyes to meet my siblings and their families. When both of my parents were finally laid to rest, my daddy decided to part ways, too. Thankfully, I had started and was committed to creating and manifesting greater from my own family no matter what showed up. So, while I mourned the loss of two fathers, I didn't allow it to break me.

The book you hold in your hands is not about my momma.

Nor is *Uplevel Your Life* about me becoming triggered to the point of potential failure when I was attaining my degree from the University of Pennsylvania. Nor is *Uplevel Your Life* about me falling down, spiraling out of control, and finding myself crying the sanctity of my soul in my sleep. If you are picking up this book and your beginnings is something you wish you could forget, this book is for you. If you know within your inner self that you have a dream in your heart and a whisper in your soul, this book is for you. And if you are inspired to seek better, pursue greater, and do more than you've ever seen or heard before, this book is for you.

You have to do some work in your mind about money, your value, your worthiness, and your ability to own your power. Regardless of what happened to you as a child, you get to choose what's best for your bank account. You must get out of the "broke" mentality that was passed on and shaken together from your mom, grandma, and your great, great, great, great grandma because that's all they knew. At the end of your day, your soul must be satisfied with whatever you name, claim, and manifest through you. I also wrote *Uplevel* in the hopes of stirring up the spark of God that resides deep on the inside. Many women—especially Kingdom and churched women— have been hurt, harmed, bruised, and scarred throughout life for too long. Similar to me prior to breaking through my hurt, trauma, and burden, most promising women bury their potential because they were cultivated to seek, know, watch, and wait for something to give them permission. Or even worse, they fail to commit to their destiny by following a dream so big that it defies everything.

As the grown version of a child who always wanted my

momma to have more, do more, and be more, I want you to permit yourself to live your best life. Even if you are/were much like me and grew up in a household that tapered your wings because your caretakers didn't know how to fly above and beyond their realities to manifest success, I am writing to you. If you have bottled up the best parts of yourself so that you don't get hurt, I want to share my story with you. Throughout *Uplevel Your Life*, you will see that I had to unlock and unleash the hidden parts within me. This book is my testimony of upleveling my mind, body, spirit, desires, and worthiness from the shadowy places to speak, seek, and seize the possibilities within me so you can see yourself in my trauma and triumphs. This book shares how you can reclaim your power, love, and have a strong mind to manifest greater for you. Throughout *Uplevel Your Life*, I want you to appreciate that you are the author, creator, finisher, and superhero of your success. No one can do you better than you!

If you are old enough to read this book, life has already shown you that Prince Charming is a farce, and Romeo will not sacrifice his hopes, dreams, or life to give you what you won't give yourself. You get to choose whether you will live the life that satisfies you or live a life that sabotages you. You get to choose whether to show up or shut yourself down. You get to choose whether to live with the labels your parents, caretakers, and the community put on you or if you will design your own labels. It's my hope that you don't settle for less than God's best. I also hope you don't become so content with the life you live that you don't seek, know, or ask for me. It is my heart's cry that you never settle, but that you allow yourself to uplevel to higher heights and deeper depths in every aspect of your life. Regardless of what you see or face, always remember you are entitled to happiness, worthy of love, and more than enough to turn your amazing destiny dreams into a reality you want to see.

Part I
Me, Myself & God

MESSY BEGINNINGS

I'll never forget my momma telling me that moments after I was born, I looked around the hospital room as if I was disappointed that she was my mother. In truth, my mom was too young to be a mother again and too free-spirited to sit still long enough to love herself, appreciate herself, or empower herself to become the woman God created her to be. Instead, she sought to be liberated from her father's home and continually concocted story after story until she became victimized by the tangled webs she weaved in an attempt to nullify the pain, sorrow, hurt, and devastation of rejection.

When I was born, I had a daddy who wasn't my biological father. True to Momma's word, she did not take another church girl's walk of shame to confess her sin of being unwed and with child. After I learned of Momma's lie, Daddy told me that he was the father I needed when Momma decided she didn't want to be a mother. He was also the father who the family court judge thought I needed when my young parents divorced less than three years after my birth. Unfortunately, or not, Momma disagreed with the family court judge when she snatched me from my home in Florida to live with her and her second husband. Within moments of meeting him, Momma made me believe he was my daddy up until she divorced him right around my 11th birthday.

While living with my stepdaddy, I didn't like the victim story of not having enough, hiding in rescue shelters for battered women, going to the food banks to get sustenance, or living with an outstretched hand, hoping someone would fill it. I always wanted to know what made the difference between those women who took their mustard seed of faith to manifest greater things and live their best life and other women who just got by. Without sound teaching, I always assumed women needed a man, a mentor, a sponsor, someone to be the hero in their story to help them defy their realities. I wasn't so obvious as to ask those I secretly studied what made them pursue greater, what shut them down, or what made them take a long break before saying goodbye.

To glean from my history, I focused on both women who affected my growth—my mother and my godmother. My birth mother was different. She had family and friends, but she lived as though apologizing for something. She had my sister and me out of the covenant of marriage. She seemed to be apologetic about some missteps and bad decisions. Besides, she didn't quite get her bearings when life pushed her into a corner and banged her head into the reality of poverty. As a result, she stopped dreaming, stopped showing up, and started to survive life. Much like many women, life sapped away her sparkle before she could live her full potential.

I didn't know then what I know now, but I knew I didn't like the life I was living. At four years old, I knew my momma's life wasn't my own. Still, no matter how hard I tried to leave her situation, I kept getting dragged back into it. When my momma married her second husband, I found myself trying to go back to the daddy I knew. Unfortunately, when I reached out through a babysitter, he didn't come for me. So, I was stuck in a situation wherein I was forced to live as someone else's daughter.

Lord knows it wasn't easy. Between the hellfire and brimstone bible studies, living in basements, and the constant yelling and screaming in the middle of the night followed by a black eye over breakfast, I wanted out. Even though I was scared of my own shadow, I decided to run away to better, greater, and more possibilities when she put me out. I wanted a different family. I wanted a different story. I wanted a new way of living. Much like the characters in the fairytales and nursery rhymes we heard as children, I knew I was a princess and not a pauper. I thought I could be like Penny and Willona in *Good Times*; my life could be amazing. I figured anything was better than where I was.

Unfortunately, I saw that Momma stopped reaching for the stars, denying herself an opportunity to live her dreams and living beneath her privileges as a welfare recipient. Momma never got to live in a house deeded to her. However, she went to church nearly seven days a week but barely manifested as the true essence of who God created her to be. We got a few glimpses of her when she bossed up and divorced her abusive husband or when she showed up in high diva fashion, but never consistently.

I didn't understand that Momma would never be able to see through my eyes because I hadn't yet been so wounded by others that I wanted to stop trying to live my version of "happily ever after" on this side of heaven. I saw Momma's potential, but I didn't know her pain. Nor did I have the words to tell her to allow yesterday's pain to pass away—to stop punishing herself for loving on men who didn't know how to love themselves or to do whatever it took to manifest pieces of heaven here on earth.

A few times, I contemplated how I could permanently escape the life I so much despised. I had attended way too many Pentecostal revivals to know that my life was not my own and that it was an unforgivable sin to cause permanent damage to your body. So, I thought about ways of "accidentally" ending my miserable life so I could free myself from wearing clothes from the Goodwill and suffering corporal punishment whenever the house was not cleaned and maintained to Momma's liking. The more I thought about the number of possibilities of ending my life, the more I imagined the effects of a botched experience. It took me a while to stop obsessing about my future end. Instead, I began reading books about lions, tigers, bears, centaurs, and unicorns. However, as I read scary, exotic books that verged on hellish to fantasy, the more I suffered from nightmares that caused me not to want to go to sleep.

I challenged the notion that I couldn't be who I wanted because of my station in life. A few times, I attempted to hide, deny, and run from my traumatized life experiences. At the age of seven, I learned to smile while choking back tears and whispers despite screaming deep down on the inside. But I never became accustomed to living beneath my possibility. Even while living in different houses, basements, and foster homes because of life circumstances, I still felt worthy of more. Even when my sisters and I were often stirred awake in the middle of the night to escape an abusive situation and find safety in a few women shelters, I never accepted the life I was forced to live as my own. When I first ran away, I was eight years old and left home after being unfairly whipped and punished for something I didn't do. I didn't have a job, an action plan, or any concrete goals, but I knew I needed to get far away from my momma and stepdaddy. So, I left with hopes of never being seen again, which was foolish since I risked my life to run away to my godmother's.

As a child, I watched my godmother part the seas of confusion, chaos, and calamity. Once she set her mind to doing something, she made plans, and as soon as she set her sights to it, she did it. When she decided to sponsor a fashion show, she did it. When she decided she was ready to get married, she did. Once she decided she wanted to move far, far away from our small town, she did. She said she was going to live her best life, and she did whatever it took to make her words matter. Because of her, I was empowered to challenge the notion that I couldn't be who I wanted to be because of the socioeconomic class I was born into. I didn't like the fact that my home was either a family member's basement, a women's shelter, a foster home, and sometimes government housing. I wanted stability. I wanted to live like other kids. I wanted to have a

Christmas filled with presents instead of having to conjure lies the day after to fabricate what I didn't receive. Much like any child with a vivid imagination, I thought I could change my life by changing my family. I wanted my regular life with my godmother to be like my weekends. Having already been through a lifetime of childhood trauma, I decided to leave in hopes of living with someone who could help me live the life I saw on television. I went to my godmother's home because she was the closest thing I had to a fairy godmother. I needed someone to rescue me from my situation, advocate for my possibilities, and keep me safe from complacency and misery. But I was returned almost as quickly as I showed up unexpectedly. My godmother's mom told her that she couldn't keep me.

When I returned to Momma's house, I focused on getting out. Believe me when I say that several switches and a few sessions with an extension cord will muzzle your voice. When the molesters showed up and put their hands in unwanted places, I said nothing. When the bullies beat me down because of my looks and high-mindedness, I acquiesced to the blows. And when I was given opportunity after opportunity to tell the social workers my truth, I said nothing. I hated my life. I had been beaten, molested, and physically abused. I became angry, quiet, and started hurting myself. The darkness of not having darkened my spirit and limited my soul. The pain of not having, not knowing, and subsisting from the breadcrumbs adultified me. Advocating for my mom to give herself and my sisters a chance to succeed despite the statistics raised something within me. Rolling my eyes when church people talked about us instilled something within me. Eventually, I stopped obsessing about what I didn't have and began focusing on what else I could do. I couldn't sing or dance, but I was super smart and a quick read on most subjects. And that's what I focused on—getting the best grades I could get so I could escape my reality. That is until I received another blow.

At or about the time I turned twelve years old, Momma told me that my stepdad wasn't really my father. She told me that I had to stop using my stepdad's last name and start using Anderson. I didn't like life with him, so it was easy to let go. Everything happened so suddenly after Momma divorced my stepdad that I was ready, willing, and able to cut him off. I didn't even flinch when I learned that my stepdad wasn't my father, nor did I ask how or why I had spent so many years as his daughter. Within six months of letting one daddy go, I met and embraced another. But my newfound connection to Daddy didn't make me want to move with him and his family down south. Instead, I had a conference call with both of my parents and requested to live with my godmother. While Momma said yes, Daddy said no. So, I was stuck trying to figure out how to live my best life in an unstable environment with Momma.

Church wasn't as welcoming either. While I was forced to attend church seven days a week, I didn't know about God's plans for me. Nor did I know about His purpose for my life. I didn't even fully appreciate how Momma lied prostrate to connect with a God she believed wanted to bless her yet lived in poverty most of her adult life. I was so disillusioned with church, pastors, and leaders that I lost my way. I wanted to live a life of abundance, walking on streets made of gold and being crowned with grace before I died. Although I gleaned Godly principles while attending church services almost seven days a week, Sunday school classes, Vacation Bible School upon high school induction, I was convinced that all divine salvation was lost since I would never be deemed as perfect under man's interpretation of God's law. So, I did what every rebellious teen does that becomes sick and tired of being sick and tired; I committed to being the opposite of Momma.

When Momma said I needed to be saved, sanctified, and a fire baptized girl to get into heaven, I became hell-bent on busting hell wide open. When Momma said I would end up in the projects just like her with a bunch of children, I committed to being celibate. When Momma said I would always be a disappointment because I just couldn't get my life together, I figured out a way to matter—even if that entailed being a menace. Unfortunately, I wound up becoming a victim of my own story. By age fifteen, I lived in several homes, including foster homes, relatives' homes, strangers' basements, and my godmother's home. When I couldn't get the stability I needed, I began to rebel so much that my godmother began to worry and suggested that Momma send me to the Milton Hershey School. Much to everyone's surprise, Momma said yes to allowing me to go to the Milt!

Part II
Manifest
Your Success

Appreciate Your Potential

While many are called to step up, step out, and be brave, most do not act for various reasons. Maybe their family wouldn't understand; their community had grown accustomed to who they are presented as, are afraid of being ignored, or worse yet, rejected. Or maybe they don't know where to begin. Even when the pain of the past has left a stench that seems too unbearable, you must force yourself to believe that your voice matters, your vision matters, and your vocation matters to someone other than you. The truth of the matter is you're not defined by what happened but by what you refuse to do about handling, healing, and helping yourself. If you don't like the last chapter, rewrite a new verse wherein you find the silver lining that can help you appreciate that you have what it takes to be great because of the greatness within you to survive this thing called life.

Through the years of trying to mold and shape myself to become the woman of my dreams, I found myself making many changes throughout the process. During my sophomore year in high school, I had an opportunity to attend Milton S. Hershey School, and the first year was hard as I had gotten expelled from two different student homes. My initial years at Milton Hershey School were not easy. In fact, I was thrown out of two students' homes within the first year because I operated in my new environment as I had operated in the very one I so desperately wanted to leave. I was so desperate to be accepted by others, I created my own *Imitation of Life* wherein Momma didn't belong. Momma made me feel guilty that I didn't want to live in the world she was forced to live. But seemingly, living in or around her shadow diminished my possibilities. I didn't want to explain the foster care and fairytale story in my new levels in life. My traumatized beginnings were nothing to brag about or share. So, I tried to pretend that none of my life existed before I arrived at Milton Hershey School.

I had grown accustomed to fighting, cursing, and hating my life throughout my childhood that I had become angry, bitter, putrid, and explosive. But my experience was more like a journey of self-realization and actualization. For the first time in my life, I was allowed to use my words, express myself, and follow my dreams. At first, I didn't realize that residue from childhood abuse and hunger had affected how I interacted with others. My induction into Milton Hershey School was not easy. Forcing an adultified girl who had to quietly suffer through molestation and find food to sustain me on more days than the law should allow is not easy. I witnessed some things that made me a perfect candidate for multiple therapy sessions by today's societal standards. I somehow felt anchored and connected to Momma's safety and sanctity, even though we were twenty years apart.

But as fate would have it, I was forced to cut the umbilical cord that tethered my soul to Momma. A few months after Momma allowed me and four of my sisters to attend Milton Hershey School, she changed her mind. Houseparent after houseparent pleaded with Momma to allow us to stay, but Momma swept in and scooped up each of her girls. When it was time for Momma to withdraw me from the school, I told Momma and my houseparents that I would not return to her. Momma had continually refused to allow me to live with my godmother, but I knew something had to change. And after living at the school for a few months wherein I slept in my own bed, ate three meals a day, and not having to live in fear of being hit with a belt, switch, or an extension cord for a small indiscretion, I knew this was my place of freedom. So, I did what I hadn't done since I was four years old, which was to advocate for myself. Before Momma agreed, she told me that I couldn't have any visitors and couldn't leave the campus until she came to get me. And that was alright with me.

My happily ever after story with my first student home was cut short after a screaming match with my housefather over oatmeal. One too many breakfasts of overcooked oatmeal at home and the women's shelter caused something within me to shudder. Unfortunately, neither I nor my housefather fully appreciated the other's position—for me to have freedom of choice and for him to limit my freedom. So, I was expelled

39

from the student home. Because I was a stellar student, I got elected to live at a student home filled with overachievers. At the second student home, I met someone I still call a friend more than thirty years later. I also met a cow that tried to kick me when I milked her. And I met another cow that caused me to slide through half a block of dung when I chased her down to get milked. Despite all the notes houseparents kept on their students, someone forgot to tell my new house family that I was a super-sassy "grown-ish" girl who was scarred by life. Anytime I felt backed into a corner, I used my mouth as both sword and shield. After five months at my second student home, I was ejected from there; they packed up my belongings while I was in class. Like the first time, I did nothing more than try to convince a white man that my thoughts mattered. But neither of my houseparents wanted to see or hear me.

In my third student home, I had to choose whether to stay mad at the world or find my own lane of success. In my defense, I wasn't a violent juvenile delinquent who had a "screw the world" mentality. I just didn't know how much anger empowered me to speak my mind when no one else would. The question of whether I wanted to stay or be expelled was emotionally heavy for me. I knew I didn't want to return home, wherein we were constantly in survival mode between the first of the month and the end of the month because of the little allotment. I also knew if I left, I wouldn't have any money to attend college because, as a first-generation college student who lived in a government house, no one saved up money to ensure we attained success. In fact, everyone figured I would learn how to survive myself.

My heart was heavy because I had played loco parentis for

so long to my younger sisters that I felt I had abandoned them. I didn't know what to do because while I was advocating for my future self, I wanted my sisters to have an opportunity to succeed, as well. I didn't have the words or the foresight to describe the inner-conflict I felt deep down on the inside. I knew the school was the best place for me. But something within me wouldn't allow others to disrespect me nor force me to be an emotional doormat just to keep the peace. At the time, I didn't even know how my upbringing had infected my spirit. While Ms. Royer essentially told me to watch what I prayed for, she acquiesced to my request to have black houseparents, but with a strong warning that I would be removed from Milton Hershey School if I couldn't get along with the houseparents. Despite the warning of expulsion, my anger button was triggered once again during an outing with my mother. Given our past encounters and my respect for my mother's position, I knew not to unleash my venom in front of my mother. In fact, throughout my stay at Milton Hershey School, one too many verbal battles with Momma almost caused me to be expelled from the very place that allowed me to be myself.

Thankfully, my final student home housemother saw the hurt and pain, but she fully appreciated the potential within me. So, instead of having me expelled from one too many instances of self-sabotage and inadvertent lawlessness on my part, she allowed me to uplevel. I chose to play by the rules by swallowing my words and putting my emotional outbreaks in a locked box. I became more mindful that the decisions I made affected whether or not I could actually live my dreams. In so doing, I was constantly checking myself to ensure I didn't allow my unconscious drifts to keep me from showing up as a better version of myself. During my senior year, I became the president of my student home, the co-editor of my school's student-run magazine, and stepped in as leader and student counselor to help other students appreciate that their actions affected their aspirations. I even took a leap of faith and applied to seven universities during my senior year and was accepted by all of them, including the University of Pennsylvania.

Eventually, I realized that my success was not contingent upon my mother's success but the decisions I made at every level of my life. I was not tethered to her, nor was she able to yank my chains. I was not my teenaged mother's mistake. I didn't force my momma to choose a father for me. Nor did I have to keep being punished for being a bastard child who didn't know her place in life. I had to find some way to uplevel my success beyond what was expected from a person who dared to go above and beyond the status quo of her possibility. Once I untethered myself from my mother's shame, I untethered myself from the shadow of my mother's possibilities. It was only then I got a chance to unleash every good thing that God spoke over me. Similarly, I want you to understand that you are not meant to replace your parents but a full manifestation of who God created you to be. You get a chance to live above and beyond your dreams. No matter your life experiences and circumstances, find a way to fully appreciate that God has a plan for you. You're not a man's mistake. You're not your mother's mistake. You're not your father's mistake. You're not your great, great, great, great, great parents' mistake either. Empower your expectations to become a better version of yourself. Believe that you are more than a conqueror. Believe that you can speak to your fear as though it is a frenemy to your soul. Believe that you can walk on the waters of your success. Believe that you can be the trailblazer of your success. Believe that you are more than an overcomer because you were a transformer. Believe so that you can rise up; believe so that you can speak up.

Transformation is hard because it is a process we must trust. We must fully appreciate that we must go through the narrow tunnel of trials, tribulations, and tests to appreciate who we are fully. We must take a walk, speak the Word, seek God's wisdom, and press through for our breakthrough. If you sit waiting for someone, you will fail to become the full epitome of who you are meant to be. Or if you allow someone to speak your word and push through for you, you will not have the strength you would have mustered from forcing yourself through the last level. No one can speak up or show up for you. You are the force majeure who is meant to catalyze change for those attached to you. The onus is upon each of you to be a better version of yourself because there is a place for you that has been carved out by the Most-High God with your name on it.

In fact, God, Divine, Universe, Higher Power—however you reference the all-being, all-knowing, and all-seeing Creator— has planned and purposed a place for you to be the force majeure of your generation. Much like Harriet Tubman, Sojourner Truth, and Dr. Martin Luther King, Jr., the presence of God is within the essence of you. But you must fully appreciate that you must move out of your way; you must trust the process and position yourself to be the walking epistle to help others appreciate that more is possible. Believe me when I say, upleveling your mind, body, and spirit to align your potential to manifest your possibilities is hard. It's so easy to blame my lack of motivation on others' failure to cultivate me. It would have been easy to hide behind the status quo, which states that more than seventy percent of people don't leave their home states, let alone their neighborhoods, during their lifetime. And unfortunately, most people don't expect children who are physically abused and molested to rise from the ashes to amass money, power, and success with desperate prayers. Whether you argue it's the nature of a person's character or an environment people come from with little to no cultivation, it is minimal elevation, if any.

But after meeting and hearing of people rising to the top on scraps of success, I gave myself a chance. Once I realized my triggers, I negated them. Once I realized there was another way to live my life, I followed the path to success. When I realized that how I survived in one environment would sabotage my growth in another, I forced myself to stop. I had to set boundaries and be intentional about building a foundation that allowed me to manifest success through myself. Similarly, you must do the same for yourself. You must assess whether you are sabotaging your growth because of what you suffered as a child. If so, remove the triggers, set your intention, and pursue a plan that allows you to manifest success at every aspect of your life on this side of heaven.

Bet on Yourself

When I first applied to the University of Pennsylvania, I didn't know the level of preparation I needed to succeed. I was a first-generation college student who was naturally gifted to pick up on the subject matter and pretty much ace the test after an hour or so of studying. But nothing I went through cultivated me to succeed in my new environment. I didn't know how to schedule my time, energy, or resources, nor did I know how to assess what was working and what was not working. Within six months of graduating from high school, I went from a distinguished honor roll to academic probation. Instead of studying and becoming acclimated to an Ivy League curriculum, I partied, drank, and pretty much sabotaged my ability to uplevel my success. The second semester of my freshman year was a little better in that

I earned enough points to continue my second year at the University of Pennsylvania. However, after the first semester of my sophomore year, I found myself on academic probation again.

It would have been easy to justify being expelled from the University of Pennsylvania by hiding behind statistics, non-support by those who should have been the most supportive. The experts are pretty much convinced that nurturance impacts whether or not a person succeeds in every aspect of their lives. My own mother wasn't committed to whether or not I actually graduated from an Ivy League school or worked as a secretary helping others pursue their dream. Pride had even kept me from seeking to know how my counselors could help me choose the right courses so that I wouldn't be so burdened by electives that wouldn't get me to my dream of becoming an attorney.

Unfortunately, the university did not ensure that I would achieve a degree. I mean, it offered an opportunity and some grant money but nothing in terms of success accountability. I could have blamed my welfare upbringing, wherein parents live days surviving life and social workers complete reports but rarely discern whether the people assigned to them are inferior, inept, or incomplete. I could have also blamed my absentee father for my failures, because a fatherless house is just as bad as a motherless one. Between the second academic probation letter and the "victim turned vixen" mentality, I was on the verge of becoming one of the three first-generation college students who was projected to drop out of college within the first two years. But while teetering on the brink of failure and possibility, I decided failure was not an option. The inner journey to your inner self allows you to fully appreciate who you are. You get to discover your strengths, likes, dislikes, weaknesses, wisdom, fortitude, possibilities, triggers, and treasurers. I recall having to face myself in the midst of taking a graduate psychology class wherein they taught Erik Erickson's Eight Stages of Development. From infancy to maturity, Erickson studied others in psychology and opined that if individuals weren't cultivated to trust themselves, be autonomous, and make decisions, they would somehow end up impaired. While the instructors were teaching from a clinical perspective, my spirit somehow awakened and persuaded my soul to listen. When both spirit and soul became aligned, I realized I was stunting my growth because broken people broke me. Between Momma muting my voice so I wouldn't tell others that she had kidnapped me or the older men who put their hands down my pants, I was persuaded not to speak the truth. In so doing, I muted my own voice and subsequently my possibilities.

The course was monumental in that I never knew one's outcomes in life were based on what was learned and experienced at every phase of our development. Seemingly, through tried and tested observation, a person's outcome was based on whether or not they were nurtured and cultivated by their parents, guardians, and/or caretakers. I wanted to prove to myself that a first-generation college student could succeed and achieve greatness. I wanted to prove to myself and others who robotically adhered to Erickson's Eight Stages of Development that anyone could achieve success if they followed their basic formula. Regardless of whether we had trust issues, self-esteem issues, or a disconnection from a strong supportive environment, I believe everyone had the wherewithal to uplevel their success. As a final paper project, I did something I had never done before, which was to assess myself similar to a scientific clinician. I needed to know for myself whether or not I was doomed to fail or if I could actually nurture myself, restore myself, and empower myself to make my dreams a reality.

As I came to realize that my traumatized self was showing up and wreaking havoc on my life, I allowed myself to evolve from the inside out. I had a lot of healing to do since I was born and shaped into shame because Momma's pregnancy with me didn't give her what she wanted, which was marriage to my father. So, Momma did what she thought she needed to create a different narrative of lies, misrepresentation, and deceit. Even when I was born, Daddy only did what he could in raising two daughters while hoping his wife would come home. When I was stabilized at around three years old, Momma snatched me and forced me to live in her new story. During childhood, I suffered because my soul forgot who I was, but my spirit wasn't okay with complacency. In my preteens, I experienced abandonment and rejection. And as I aged, the spirit of worthlessness manifested from me until I became aware of how I was sabotaging myself.

Unfortunately, my newfound self-awareness did not prevent me from playing around with my future. Instead, I continually did what I had always done, which was try to get in and fit in so I wouldn't get kicked out. Eventually, my "robbing Peter to pay Paul" short-sightedness caught up with me in that I didn't have enough points to stay in the Ivies. But after living the life I lived and upleveling my life experiences,

I refused to go back to struggle and deficiency. I saw how others lived, and I wanted the opportunity to live as they did. In a last-ditch effort to avoid going back to the very place I attempted to run from, I began asking people I partied with how they maintained a decent GPA. Much to my surprise, everyone conceded that success left clues. One party animal after another advised that they studied just as much as they partied to ensure they attained the requisite grades. So, I did what once came naturally to me, which was to study like my life was dependent upon it.

At the end of the semester, I was shy of the requisite points I needed to pass to my junior year. I was so close that something within me was activated, and I knew I had to give myself permission to prosper regardless of my previous mistakes and mishaps. I went back to all of my teachers and asked them for a grade change or at least an opportunity to retake my final exam. The first teacher listened to me and seemed to have heard my pleas, but said no and gave me a lecture on taking school seriously. The second teacher dismissed me without ever acknowledging my request. The third and fourth were just as terse, and I almost gave up on myself. But nothing beats a try other than an ask. So, I took the leap of faith and asked. Much to my surprise, my Abnormal Psychology professor (go figure) said yes, but he only gave me a weekend to learn everything I needed to know to retake the exam with one condition. The condition was that my grade would be changed to whatever I needed to have enough points to remain at the University of Pennsylvania. Needless to say, I ignored anything and everything that came against me and my goal of manifesting passing to my junior year.

Never underestimate the power of focused intensity, because you will do what you never thought you could do to achieve your dreams. After passing the examination, I showed myself that I was more than enough to succeed at whatever level. By refusing to absently take in another's negativity, I bolstered my ability to stop listening to my critical inner voice of fear and doubt. In fact, I changed the voice that always reminded me of what I couldn't do, persuading it that more was possible. I stopped focusing on my wounds and started focusing on my wins. I stopped focusing on what others did to hurt me and started focusing on what I could do to help myself. I allowed myself to win by seeing myself win. In so doing, I positioned myself to have more, do more, and achieve success. I didn't wait for anyone to magically wave a wand. Instead, I made my dreams a reality, and I did the work.

Similarly, you must refuse to lose. No matter what you did to sabotage yourself, give yourself permission to go beyond welfare, welts, bruises, failures, and disillusionment. Don't allow yourself to stay in the gutters of society or live within the shadows of your possibility. No matter who doesn't help, who won't help, who will never support, and who will only see you as a traumatized child, hopeless victim, promiscuous woman, utter failure, or worthless sinner, give yourself permission to be better today than you could have ever been. Be the new thing. Be the woman of your dreams, and be your best friend by positioning yourself to be the person who allows you to prosper. When you are given an opportunity to live, love, and achieve bigger, greater, and more than you've ever seen or heard before, take it. Don't just try it out, either! Instead, commit to the dream and advocate for your future possibilities. Never forget you are blessed and a child of God who has the power, love, and a strong mind to become the best version of yourself. Allow the words of your mouth and the meditations of your heart to lead and direct you to a better version of yourself.

As long as you are not expecting anything, you will not elevate yourself. As long as you are not expecting anything, you will subconsciously accept what shows up in life. So, stop expecting the worst thing that can happen. Stop expecting that no one is going to love you, accept you, or fully appreciate you. You must be your own advocate.

You must set your own boundaries to ensure you don't offer your pearls to swine. Even if you find yourself serving as your one and only cheerleader, seek better for you. Embrace and nurture the best part of you to emerge as the fullest version of yourself. No matter how much your heart aches for acceptance, bet on yourself. Don't dimmer your shine or play small because others don't fully appreciate the game of life. Instead, double down on your blessings until you defy your reality. You must empower yourself to be the Most Valuable Person in your entire life.

Give yourself permission to reach for the goals. Give yourself permission to win by any means necessary. Give yourself permission to defy the status quo. Go to school. Say yes to the job. Create the business. Buy and sell shares that help you enlarge your territory. Give yourself permission to go up the social ladder, climb the corporate ladder, and then make your own ladder. Take a leap to change the trajectory of your destiny. Don't be the saboteur of your success because no one lets you be the woman of your dreams. Bet on yourself so much that you empower and position yourself in front of people, places, and things no one in your family has ever seen or heard before. While most people don't even get started, don't be like them. Be the woman you need to be to empower yourself to uplevel your success.

Unlock the greatness within you that is more than enough to become unstoppable. Be the trailblazer who doesn't give up because life is hard or no one supports you. Allow yourself to rework what didn't work. Remind yourself that the race isn't given to the swift or the strong. Always remember that quitters never win. Know that you have to be fruitful and multiply. Be so committed to succeeding that you give yourself permission to fulfill your destiny by stepping up, speaking up, and showing up for every good thing you feel God planned and purposed for you.

Make Room for Grace

I wish someone had told me that it was okay to be different. I wish someone gave me permission to be bold. I wish someone told me that wanting to touch the sky was divine. And I wish someone told me that the best thing in life was to make my dreams a reality. Unfortunately, no one told me that I could live my dreams. No one told me that you must "faith" it to make it, and no one ever told me that my uniqueness qualified me to stand in my "enoughness". No one could tell me what I needed to hear, teach me how to fly, or be comfortable with asking why. *Why can't I? Why won't I?* They were questions often shushed away. You see, those who heard my questions learned firsthand that girls who asked questions were deemed as troublemakers, or worse yet, castigated or ostracized to living a life outside the lines of social acceptance.

Because no one told me that I had been selected, elected, or commissioned by God to live my best life, I went to church but did not develop a relationship with Him. At one point in my life, I started expecting setbacks instead of appreciating that setbacks allowed me to step back and shift my focus to get up and begin again. Some setbacks made me fall, such as my mistaken beliefs in finding love in the dimpled one, the undercover betrothed one, and the one who had too much pain in his life that he didn't have room in his heart for me. But that didn't mean I didn't try again and again and again until I finally realized my foolishness in thinking that a kiss from pure love could transform toads into my Prince Charming.

Most people say they don't want to share their business with others, but not sharing will cause another to lose hope and faith in better tomorrows. I spent too much of my life trying to fit in where I didn't belong, trying to pretend that I was happy, fine, content, and satisfied so people wouldn't judge me, mock me, or completely ignore me. Unfortunately, without guidance, I became sad, then mad, and then uncontrollable in trying to appease a spiritual hunger that was indescribable. I tried everything to fill the innate need that grew larger when I no longer wanted to appease. Before I knew it, I didn't even recognize myself—my face, my dreams, my desires, my plans, or even the life I aspired to achieve.

However, while seriously considering ending myself, my spirit awakened, which allowed me to appreciate that I had the power to rewrite my story. Maybe I could become my mantra so much so that I would begin to imagine what happily ever after looked like. At first, I tried to do whatever I could to get others to see me, hear me, and notice me by doing differently.

Unfortunately, after many do-overs, false starts, and restarts, I no longer loved myself enough to try. After living in negativity, being used and abused, judged, and put on the back burner because "I was acting out" and "asking for too much", something within me spun out of control. You see, I tried to get in and fit in so that others didn't notice my faults and deficiencies. But even though I tried to be who I thought others wanted me to be, it wasn't good enough for them. Rejection after rejection after rejection, I became who those I wanted to love me rejected. And I went full out. I began spewing venom and allowing hatred to fester in me; I became dark. I was a pretty face but a pretty mess.

During that time of darkness, I lost longtime friends, went through lovers, was fired by a few employers, and avoided mirrors because I couldn't stand who I had become. I had reached a new level of brokenness wherein all that I knew myself to be was removed. Aside from my independence, my degrees, and my various jobs and responsibilities, I had nothing. I didn't even have my drug-dealer guy who made me feel special with all of his scars, his children's mothers, and potential power to make me or break me because he let me go. And after he left me, I felt so rejected that I wanted to end it all. But my Pentecostal upbringing eliminated any options of doing wrong with my body. Instead, I prayed to see another side of heaven. Loneliness and inherited depression will skew one's perception so much that you only see problems, pain, confusion, chaos, and negativity. In my distress, I asked for an intervention to remove my unhappiness.

Some would call it a Divine Intervention, others a Holy Instant. Whatever you call it, that one encounter changed the trajectory of my destiny. One day while I was sleeping, I had a dream wherein my spirit travailed for me. My spirit wept, wailed, and prayed throughout the night because it wanted to live. I tossed, turned, and cried in my sleep because something had a hold of me. My spirit literally prayed that I could appreciate my significance, potential, and possibilities. By way of transparency, I literally prayed, "God, please let me get sick so I can wake up on the other side of heaven." Thankfully, God looks after babies and fools, and He refused to listen to my prayers of allowing me to get so sick that I died in my sleep. Instead, God allowed me to pray for myself at or about the time I felt like I was so dirty that I wouldn't allow myself to enter into a church to request prayer for my soul.

I'll never forget dreaming a prayer many years ago wherein I saw myself travailing as the older women did during spirit-led revivals. During the prayer, my spirit was crying out for my heart, my mind, my soul; I was pleading the blood of Jesus and asking God to help me see the real me. Unbeknownst to me, my spirit prayed on my behalf so that I could uplevel beyond my realities to truly appreciate my limitless possibilities. The dream felt so real to me that I sweated out of my nightclothes, had tears in my eyes, and my spirit felt so drained as though I had prayed all night long to intercede for myself. Lies of men, rejection of women, dreams never fully lived, and living from paycheck to paycheck made me feel as though God was done with me. But my spirit wasn't ready to throw in the towel. Much like what it did for me when I started making arrangements to move back to Harrisburg, the Holy Spirit allowed me to appreciate that I could work out my own salvation with fear and trembling. I could turn my life around and write the script of my destiny, or I could wait for someone to rescue me. I wasn't a damsel in distress; I could do something to help me have more, do more, and be more all by myself.

The next day happened to be a Sunday, and I made a decision to go to church. I didn't know where I was going, I didn't have church clothes, nor did I know anyone at the church. But I went to the church that happened to be seven blocks from my house until my soul was persuaded more was possible. Once I realized I was entitled to love, worthy of happiness, and more than enough to live my dreams, I began setting boundaries. I began making demands on myself, and I began setting the intentions to become the woman of my dreams. To manifest success, you must make room for grace. God doesn't care what you have been through, where you have been, and what you did or didn't do. God will continually chasten to change his children so that we can manifest greater here on Earth. We only see what we see and determine what's next from our one perspective and/or position.

I wanted to live my version of 'happily ever after' on this side of heaven. I no longer wanted to live by doing as others, but I wanted to be who I was. I no longer worried about whose child I was or wasn't, but I just wanted to show up like me without feeling any guilt, bondage, and without explanation or permission because of my humble beginning. I just wanted to be better than I had ever been without the need to lose or give myself away as I did before. So, after years of starting, stopping, running on empty, and starting the cycle all over again, I did the unthinkable and asked God to help me become the woman of my dreams. I wanted to live the life I chose. I wanted to handle negativity and defeat as though it was nothing more than an inconvenience, and I wanted to invite God in to see me, hear my heart, and help me become a better version of myself despite my past mistakes, missteps, and misunderstandings. Thankfully, between my dreams serving as a talisman to enlighten the path of my soul or the Holy Spirit provoking my spirit, I somehow found a way to protect my hope to live above and beyond my tears, fears, spiritual wounds, and life circumstances. Lord knows it was a lot of trials, trauma, rejection, and other people's misdirection and manipulation. But after getting through the shadows that were born from the residue of generational trauma, the truth made me appreciate this one thing above everything.

When you make room for grace, you will come to a place in your life wherein life as you know it will change. You'll discover the answer to that nagging question about whether you are meant for more. You will also get the insight you need to erase or embrace a committed relationship. You will find yourself on a path that is the stark opposite of your comfort zones. In making room for grace, your voice is clear, your judgment is sound, your passion is contagious, and you are inspired to live more, love more, and do more. And when you choose to share, it's no longer burdensome but actually a natural response to God's goodness, mercy, and grace. Once you are committed to becoming who God created you to be, another's judgment doesn't matter. Another's deception doesn't matter. Another rejection doesn't matter. Another deceit doesn't matter, and another's harsh words don't matter. The only thing that matters is protecting your spirit from that of the world in order to become the miracle you were meant to be.

Your inner self also becomes open to the possibility that your eyes may not have seen it all, and your ears may not have heard all of those good things God has in store for you. You allow yourself to become more open to any shifts in the atmosphere and less tolerant of the same ole same ole or the status quo. Even when others are willing to wait, be still, or be complacent in their circumstance, do not be like them. Follow your desire by pressing forward to the rhythmic cadence of your beating heart. Your cadence is yours and is not based on another's barking orders, compulsive behavior, or limitations. It is controlled by you. Each day, share with others your inner brilliance that shines brightly deep down on the inside and that is fueled by your hopes, dreams, inspiration, motivation, and inner desire to become more.

Empower Your Expectations

Life may not be fair, nor is it predictable, but it consistently responds to those who have the courage to allow themselves to step up, step out, and show up for better, greater, and more opportunities to live their dreams. Throughout my life, I have always wanted to see how life responded to those who weren't pretty enough, smart enough, rich enough, or liked enough by people who knew people. I needed life to make a way somehow for the poor kids who were traumatized by life experiences and circumstances but weren't talented enough to get on television or skinny enough to be picked up by the top modeling company or even popular enough to catch the eye of those in the community who seemingly wave a wand and make the least expected desirable enough to become somebody.

I needed something in my life that would help me transform my beginning story to my happily ever after without getting hurt by negativity, defeat, strife lessons, and strongholds that continually showed up every time I tried to uplevel my life. Just as many individuals believe their spirits were placed into the wrong body, I felt that somehow, the Divine had accidentally put me with the wrong family. Every time I demanded bigger, better, and more, I was shot down. Every time I questioned the urban class system of the have and have nots, I was shot down. And every time I demanded to learn how to sing, dance, and act so that I could get into pageantry for the chance to receive scholarships, I was shot down. I had a plan to get from where I was to where I needed to be, but I needed the money to learn a skill or something to get someone to appreciate that I was worthy of being the person I dreamed of, hoped for, and prayed for. But each time I pushed to be like others, talk like others, walk like others, and do as others, I was shot down.

I thought happily ever after was a person, place, or thing instead of something that could be manifested. Because of the limited knowledge about who I was and the potential for greatness I had within myself, I just thought if I were pretty or smart enough, my Prince Charming would save me from the things and people that made my life a living hell. But Prince Charming didn't come fast enough for me, nor did the recording contracts, modeling contracts, or anything else that could help me get away from the life I knew. I did what others do without a plan, purpose, and goal; I found myself scratching and surviving life, asking God to escape entanglements throughout life, and barely being fulfilled in life.

I had no clue I was making judgments about what's best for me based on what others presented and told me. I wanted to live my version of 'happily ever after' on this side of heaven. I no longer wanted to live by doing as others. I wanted to be who I was. I no longer worried about whose child I was or wasn't, but I wanted to show up like me without feeling any doubt, guilt, or resentment because of my humble beginnings. I just wanted to be better than I had ever been before without the need to lose myself or give myself away as I did before. As I took the initial leap of faith, I realized that faith empowers everyone to manifest the things they hoped for based on what they seek, what they speak, and what they need. Faith makes anyone who believes in themselves an outlier. In actuality, faith is the substance of things hoped for, prayed for, wished for, and the evidence that good things happen to those who believe in themselves.

To live your best life, you must take charge of it by seeking better, pursuing greater, and doing more. You must level up your heart, mind, and understanding to higher heights and deeper depths. You must seek to see beyond your reality, your life experiences, and circumstances. You must appreciate the power within you to manifest greater from you. If you want to see what you've never seen before or hear what you've never heard before, you must do what you've never done before. Unfortunately, nothing changes if nothing changes. But when you decree, declare, design, and do whatever it takes to live the life of your dreams, better things are manifested through you.

If you're anything like me who was waiting to be rescued, I'm sure you found yourself waiting for someone to turn your dreams into realities. I'm also sure you've found yourself dimming your shine so that others could appreciate their own spark. Unfortunately, most women are cultivated to wait for our prince to find us. Nor can church girls escape the fairytale delusion since we often hear the overly quoted scripture, "He who finds a wife finds a good thing." Well, I was deemed as a good thing despite my messy beginning. Someone asked me to run their children and newsletter ministry, yet I felt empty and shallow. It took me accidentally seeing my red, puffy face from too many nights of uncontrollable, heartfelt sobbing that welled from the pain of living a life that I didn't love. I didn't want to continually live a life of tears, so I decided to find a way to stop crying. The pain of not having and not seeing what I wanted for myself became so great that I found myself doing something to change it. Well, a sister shooting herself and me almost dying from an ectopic pregnancy woke me up to the fact that life would go on with or without me.

After realizing that life is what I make it, I stopped blaming the folks who didn't know better, and I started imagining what life could look like if I actually made better decisions for myself. I started imagining going on vacation to pleasure islands and began making plans to visit. I started imagining that I had money in the bank and started making plans to have what I saw. I started imagining wearing my dream size and started making lifestyle changes to get there. The onus is upon us to become who God created us to be. You must understand that God planned and purposed a special place on you on this side of heaven. There is a space for you. There is a place for you that is etched in your soul, but you must go through the trauma to become triumphant. You must go through the variations of victimhood to fully appreciate your power to live in victory. And yes, you must go through misery to manifest greater success, and you're going to have to go through the process of elimination. To achieve greater, you must seek the specialness about you within you.

Find the place within your heart that gives you strength to be the best version of yourself. The power within you gives you strength to be fruitful, multiply, and dominate in every aspect of your life. Position yourself to be a better version of yourself. Find a way to ask God for insight so you can see what you need to see. Seek to see the people, places, and things that will help you uplevel out of the survival mentality so you can unleash your limitless possibilities. Force yourself to imagine what's possible. Imagine yourself living a destiny that nurtures your dreams and defines your reality. Stop trying to fit into manmade structures, and give yourself permission to see the path that fulfills you. Allow yourself to find a way to manifest success at new levels. Once you fully understand who you are, whose you are, and your capacity to defy your reality, you won't stay stuck trying to be who you aren't. What I know for sure, we all have something that we're designed to do. Regardless of what happened, what didn't happen, who diminishes you, who denied you, or who tried to play you, you still matter. In fact, you are a walking, talking, living, loving, brilliant and beautiful miracle. Your personality, your idiosyncrasies, your beliefs, your goals, and your visions all matter, right?

Take a moment to appreciate that you have what it takes to be successful. You don't always have to merely survive in the life that you are more than enough to shine in. You don't even have to get by because others do. You get a chance to thrive in a life you love. You don't have to deny yourself, but you need to look around and see what the successful people do. When you realize what successful people do, you realize there is a time and a place for everything, and within everything, there is a time and a place. There is a promise for you to be promoted, but you have to go through the process of becoming a better version of yourself. Remove your scarcity mentality. Remove anything that keeps you reimagining living the life you want, desire, and love. Get out of the "woe is me" mentality because we all have had a "woe is me" mentality.

Appreciate that God has given you the purpose, passion, and potential to live, love, and have your being in the very spaces and places that your ancestors could never imagine. Allow yourself to be the trailblazer of your success—the new thing. Believe more is supposed to be manifested through you that you find a way to defy your ancestor's dreams. Be more than the status quo of scratching and surviving. Be the force majeure. Be the one God can use to help you and your family have bigger, better, and more breakthroughs. Position yourself to be a better version of yourself. Position yourself to seek greater days. Position yourself to have more, do more, and be more to turn your big, amazing, destiny-driven and audacious dreams into a reality.

Be Your Own Rescue

There comes a time in everyone's life wherein an inexplicable craving will show up that can't be appeased by the same ole same ole. At first, you'll try to suppress the hunger and thirst for more with something you know, but it won't be good enough. You might even reach out to family and friends in an effort to understand what's happening to you. You may even try to determine what, if anything, they would suggest for you to do. But eventually, their chatter won't be good enough. You might even go to a church and sit on the pews in hopes of hearing something to inspire you to do something about this insatiable appetite that seemingly roars like a lion both day and night, but ultimately what you hear won't be good enough.

Regardless of how low or high you go to appease your

insatiable appetite, or whether you choose to ignore it, nothing will be good enough. Regardless if you try to appease it with drugs, money, sex, or degrees, nothing will be good enough. In fact, you may find yourself running out of options in an attempt to appease your craving. Eventually, you'll have no other choice but to be still long enough to fully appreciate that the craving for more stems from you. Now whether you allow the whimper to turn into a roar before you submit to the process of satiating your appetite from the inside out, you'll eventually be forced to the process of dealing with the cravings within you.

After being loosened from the spirit of complacency and mediocrity that possessed so many of my ancestors, I had made a few changes in my life. More specifically, I began attending a Bible-teaching church to hear the sermon. I also stopped giving my number to the drug dealers, panty pushers, and church hustlers who could only appreciate my big butt and smile. And I'm sure several wives were thankful I stopped wearing thigh-high spandex skirts that barely covered my goodies. I also sorta, kinda, maybe stopped cursing people out whenever they got on my last nerve. I also started making plans to create the life I loved no matter what. Trust me when I say the battle for your soul is real. The universe truly conspires against you so much so that most of us stop ourselves before we even begin. Or worse yet, we unconsciously speak negativity into our existence instead of speaking what we need to fulfill a greater destiny. Many of us are spiritually wounded by what others did or didn't do for us during our childhood. Because we can't see the scars, we act like they don't exist. But the core of the scar lies deep.

Unfortunately, the pain of not having, doing, or becoming stunts our growth.

What do you do when you are loosened, but stuck between reality and destiny? What do you do when you no longer want to be a WAG and long to be a WOG, but you're judged based on who you used to be? What do you do when you no longer want to survive life but create the life you love? What do you do when your spirit continually battles with a victim mentality that was molded and shaped by negativity? These were the questions that plagued my spirit after I took a leap of faith to change the trajectory of my destiny. The love you want, need, and desire is within you. You see, I never knew the value of my voice, my vision, and my worth. I never knew it for a long time because I was living in the shadow of my possibilities. I mean, let's be real. When you are on the poor side of being poor, you don't have many options. Even when I was living a life that I hated, I was hoping and praying for my own version of Prince Charming to take me far, far away from my reality. I was looking for someone to hold me, love me, sacrifice for me, and save me. I needed someone to need me, but I didn't know that someone first had to be me. It could have been an old man. It could have been a drug dealer. It could have been a baller shot caller. I didn't care who was going to rescue me. No matter how much I prayed for someone to pick me, love me, protect me, adopt me, rescue me, it wasn't going to happen.

I even thought that if I hooked up with rich people, older people, or even drug dealers, I could live a good life. I mean, anything was better than living in basements and shelters. I thought anyone was better than being seen but not heard or heard but not appreciated. After heartbreak after heartbreak hoping for a soul mate, I finally met a guy who looked like he needed and appreciated me. He went to church, was educated, handsome, and a great lover. But I didn't realize his heart wasn't available. He was scared of commitment because he had been scarred throughout his life. He also didn't trust women because the women he previously trusted had ripped out his heart. I gave him the best that I had. I gave him my heart, mind, and body. What he gave me in return was a warm bed, great conversations, and a glimmer of what love could look like if two individuals were willing to let go of the pain to live a life of peace, joy, and happiness.

I was traumatized because I met a good guy, but I lost him. Then I found my rescuer, who happened to be a well-known and violent drug dealer. It's kind of funny when you're looking for something, you eventually find it. But my rescuer was a very sweet and sensitive drug dealer guy. He had a brand-new car with leather seats. He smelled good. He had a warm heart. He had a firm grip and hug. That's what I needed at that time. I needed someone to love me. And he would tell me, I have a lot of kids, and his pager would always go off. It was kind of weird, but I didn't care because, for the first time, he wasn't even asking me for sex. He listened to my dreams and my goals and the aspirations of what I was going to do. But he let me go because I had the potential.

I didn't know I had the power within me to change my life story. I had been lied to and denied so many times that I stopped reimagining the possibilities of what could be. I can't say I was miserable because surviving is not dying. But life became frustrating as I showed up as an empty vessel looking for someone to take my hurt away. When that void is not filled by something, the foundation of our cascade begins to crack. As I saw the cracks in my heart, mind, and foundation, I tried to fill them with something—boys, men, school, a job that sapped my energy, or even mindless television. Eventually, even the very things that helped me ignore my frustration became annoying and also unavoidable, so much that I needed an escape that would allow my soul to sleep.

What is often not mentioned but must be understood is that our lives may not be our own, but we must make our dreams, life vision, and goals a priority. If we don't make our aspirations and inspiration a priority, the past will continually be successful at keeping us at the status quo by strangling our potential. We are what we see, and we often seek what we need. Yet, we fail to seek to objectify ourselves as a people to know who we are and what we've achieved and accomplished despite our experience and circumstances. It is always interesting that most of us live as though we are experiencing life as trailblazers instead of appreciating and acknowledging that there is nothing new under the sun. People will treat you the way you treat yourself.

Accordingly, you must fully appreciate who you are. You must fully appreciate your voice, vision, and values. You must advocate for yourself. You must nurture and cultivate yourself. If you want to uplevel your money game, you must bankroll your brilliance. If you want to live as though you are blessed and highly favored, you must believe you are. If you want to see bigger, greater, and more than you've ever seen or heard before, you must set the intention. No matter how much you may want someone to pick you up, turn you around, and place your feet in the place of your dreams, it's not going to happen.

No good thing will happen until you tap into the greatness within you.

Once you begin to take the time to seek, know, and ask how to satisfy yourself, you'll see that greater is within you more than outside of you. Similar to infants learning to move on their own for the first time, you will also find yourself during this discovery period enamored at hearing your voice saying "no" to what no longer suits you. You'll also be shocked to find yourself standing on your own two feet and walking away from people, places, and things that hurt you more than help you. As you continually seek to see what else you can do for yourself, you'll eventually discover what's in you— greatness. And once you learn that you were fearfully and wonderfully made to be great all by yourself, just enough and barely enough will no longer be good enough for you. Instead, you will find yourself living, loving, and becoming your own breakthrough so much so that you rescue yourself from being a victim of a story you were never meant to live.

Push Through Your Pain

Ioften think about how we deal with lessons we were forced to learn. I mean, we all have a past we can ignore, embrace, or learn from. However, when we ignore the past, it stunts our growth, and it continuously comes back with a vengeance until it's dealt with. Similarly, unlearned lessons we try to ignore are used to serve as excuses to explain away why we aren't quite where we want to be or meant to be. In contrast, when we deal with our past by objectifying it, we empower ourselves to free ourselves from its stronghold. We empower ourselves to flex our faith, which helps us grow our confidence. We also allow ourselves to get through the lesson that we can use in making new decisions for new dimensions.

Some may argue with me, but in general, we become what we see and do what other people do. So, if we saw people pray a lot, we more than likely repeat what we saw. If we saw people fight a lot, we will more than likely become fighters. And if we saw people curse people, our natural inclination may be to curse someone out before we think about the hurtful words that come out of our mouths. Unfortunately, we become who we are because of other people's choices and perceptions.

Opportunities come and go, but the key to upleveling your mind, vision, mission, and money is to believe more is possible. NEVER get so beat down by life that you fail to look up. Look up to seek God's insight despite what's inside. Go to the source of your injury by taking inventory of your past pains—the things that hurt you the most year-by-year, if you must. You need to access that information because you need to eject it from your mind, body, and spirit. Once you identify that very poison that has kept you stuck, you will become a lot more effective at becoming who you are meant to be. What I really want you to do is to go a little deeper until you tap into your true feelings. Identify how you felt; live in your feeling until you ignite your spirit and fuel your soul.

If the pain didn't affect who you are, assess to see if you have grown from it. Believe me when I say how shocked I was to learn that my age had gotten older, but my spirit did not grow. For many years, I was operating as the traumatized girl who was tip-toeing in my existence instead of showing up as the fullness of who I am. I didn't realize my soul had stopped growing after being hit time and time again with spiritual missiles. Once I realized during a self-help conference that my soul's age and my spirit's age were years apart, I took hold of what kept me stuck. When I delved into the painful memories, I saw the areas I had gotten stuck in and also the places I needed to grow into. Once I got clear on the painful areas, I was also able to identify the painful ones.

We must find the beauty in the scars that serve as reminders of what we healed from. Even though some people cut us so deep for no reason, we not only survived, but the marks left behind serve as reminders of how far we came. The scars serve as reminders that deep down on the inside there is something greater that helps us overcome hurt, pain, sickness, and disease. In allowing your scars to serve as beauty scars, you are reminded of what could have killed your spirit but didn't. You are even reminded of what could have held your hope as a hostage to your realities but didn't. And your scars can serve as a token of God's love that reminds you that God went through with you. Take a look at your scars to appreciate that He never left you or forsake you—He merely served as your shield, protector, strong tower, and waymaker through all of it.

God led and guided you even when you didn't appreciate the tugging on your heart or the whispers in the dark. He loves you, needs you, and will restore you to your rightful place as his child. Give God all of your hurt, pain, abuse, and confusion. Release your frustration, fear, tears, and disappointment into the atmosphere. The pain of who you were yesterday made you who you are today, refined who you are today, but does not define who you are today. Letting go doesn't mean it did not affect you, because it really did, or you wouldn't have held on to it for so long. But letting go allows you to heal from the heavy burden of carrying it, reliving it, and dealing with it. Letting go thus makes it insignificant to who you are today.

Your yoke is easy, and your burden is now light because the heavy emotional baggage has been released. You have to let go to receive because a clenched fist gets nothing, while an open palm allows you to receive everything. Regardless of what's insight, seek to see through the eyes and spirit of Christ that overcame the scars, the scorn, the hate, the misunderstanding, and all of the hell He was forced to live through. If He could do it, you can do greater just as He promised so long as you pray in His name. Whatever you ask for and believe, you shall see that and more abundantly. So, if you want God in your present situation, speak him into your atmosphere—in your homes, your jobs, your churches, your comings, and your goings.

How you react to any situation is based on your willingness to protect yourself from all hurt, harm, danger, negativity, and deceit because you make your life a priority. Once you realize that you were fearfully and wonderfully made on purpose, then you begin to seek knowledge to gain a better understanding of who you are and what you offer as an expert of your experience. You become wiser at making better decisions to live, love, and become who you're meant to be. The journey of becoming will not be easy because you must first conquer an inner struggle within yourself. Whatever you want for tomorrow, you must become skillful at molding and shaping what comes your way today. Whatever you went through would be in vain if you don't firmly focus on living your best life no matter what shows up.

Although cultivated to do so, you don't have to get in to fit in the world that you were born into. If it were so, God wouldn't have commanded you to seek the Kingdom that is etched into the fabric of your soul. Nor are we supposed to try to get in and fit into the mind valleys of our neighborhoods, church halls, communities, or with the poor and righteous teachers who only know how to parrot what they heard more than live out their best life. The best thing you can ever do for yourself is to love yourself enough to give yourself permission to live your dreams. Living your best life is less about getting it right the first time and more about appreciating that when you walk by faith and not by sight, everything is going to be alright.

Each day offers new mercies, new blessings, and new opportunities to Relax, Relate, and Revise your life story. Even when people laugh at your dreams, give yourself permission to believe more is possible. Even when your realities don't look like your destiny, give yourself permission to believe more is possible. Even when no one supports you, give yourself permission to step out on faith to do whatever it takes to be the difference-maker in your life. I'm sure the idea of giving yourself permission to go beyond your beyond is hard to fathom, especially when you may have tried once, twice, or several times before. But if you don't push yourself to live your best life, you never will. If you don't follow God's whispers, you'll never fulfill God's purpose for your life. If you wait for the perfect timing, you may miss out on God's blessing that shows up when you least expect it.

Whether you were deemed as a failure, or even worse, your parents' mistake, you can upgrade your station in life. Whether you are two steps away from bankruptcy or nickel-and-diming yourself to maintain a status quo, you have everything you need to come out of that situation. Even if you find yourself continually on your knees instead of walking by faith on your own two feet, you don't have to stay there. You need only to upgrade your mind to fully appreciate that you do not have to stay where you are.

You must seek to know your truth. Who are you at the core of who you are? What is your mission in life? Where do you hope to be? What do you crave? What drives you crazy? And what keeps you stuck in the midst of complacency and sameness? Be very clear about your answers because, at the end of the day, you must fully appreciate who you are in order to mold, shape, and unleash yourself as the most valuable version of yourself. If you don't know the basic answer to who you are, what you want, and how you will achieve it, you'll continue to live beneath your divine privileges. You will fall for those who offer sizzle and then fizzle within the same season. You will look for pieces of heaven outside of yourself, and you will step up and out from time to time but fail to make progress.

You don't transform overnight into the best version of yourself. However, when you give yourself a chance to rewrite your life story, you discover and appreciate the core of who you are. Once you start believing in yourself, you will better advocate for yourself. You will start positioning yourself to show up for success. You will stop allowing emotional vampires to suck you dry. You will set boundaries around your heart's desires. If you are anything like me, you need to see that you are not alone. You need to see that someone just like you went beyond their beyond, got scarred, got scared, and then forced themselves to start all over again. You must test the process to see if anyone besides you has made progress.

Unfortunately, if you continually do what you've always done, you will get the same results. But if you allow yourself to be still for a moment, determine how you want to live, what you are willing to do to achieve it, and be willing to commit to it, then you will have a standard to live by and have others abide by. When you want more, ask for more, expect more, and seek more. Never decrease your standard for anything or anyone, because you are a queen who is worthy of love, respect, joy, peace, and happiness. So, if love becomes a battlefield or you become frustrated about your living circumstances or situations, then it's time to move on. Just know, the things you most want are not given but revealed, claimed, and protected by you.

Recreate Your Story

You are God's masterpiece. He knew you before you were a twinkle in your mother and father's eyes. God gave you a purpose before you breathed air on this side of heaven. Much like a crumbled one-million-dollar check, you are worthy and valuable to your Maker. As long as you are breathing, God is giving you enough time to become a vessel he can use to be the answer to someone's prayer, to serve as the force majeure of ancestral trauma, and to be the wealth catalyst in your family. Despite your realities, you must become the fullness of who God created you to be. Much like an acorn to an oak tree, your value and your potential are undeniable.

Even if you were accidentally seeded into your mother's wound, you are meant to be. If you had more bad days than good days, you can control the narrative. Even if you ask for forgiveness more than most people will allow, forgive yourself for not having, not doing, not becoming the full epitome of who you believe you can be. Don't get messed up so bad that you don't find a way to become the Master's Piece. Believe me when I say that I was messy. I lied, I cheated, and I played pretense games. Life had gotten so bad that I was willing to allow anyone to become my rescuer so long as they helped me get far, far away from my realities.

Look at yourself in the mirror and remind yourself that you're responsible for creating and recreating your story. Without question, you are ultimately responsible for becoming the fullness of who God says you are. When we get knocked down by life—lose a job, a spouse, a business, or a dream, we let negativity and defeat speak for us instead of faith and expectations. But even after a knockdown drag-out fight, you are still who you were BEFORE the fight, and unless you die, you will see another day. So, the ultimate question is whether you will hide and deny yourself after the loss or if you will show up each day believing, owning, seeking, and seizing another opportunity to get what's yours.

In order to purposefully uplevel to higher heights and deeper depths in every aspect of your life, you must appreciate that God wants you to prosper in your mind, body, spirit, relationships, and finances. Most of us do not know our power because we were not taught about our power, the source of our power, or the purpose of our power. Instead, our power lies dormant while we live our lives as hearers, doers, and waiters. As children, we often heard that we should sit down, shut up, sit pretty, sit quietly, and act nice. In response, most of us grew up hoping that we somehow could matter to someone other than ourselves. In effect, we did for others more than we did for ourselves. We sat pretty for others; we received awards, competed for trophies, created the right sound, wore the right clothes, and even diminished our shine. By constantly hearing and continually doing, we unconsciously allowed our ego to take control of our lives. And when the ego takes over, we can never be good enough to do anything. In effect, analysis paralysis and the spirit of comparison will keep us from becoming who God created us to be.

Even when we obtain more material possessions, attain more degrees and certifications, live in the right zip code, socialize with the right social, or possess the most coveted spiritual anointing, we somehow find fault in our fabulosity. As we eliminate Godly options by counting ourselves out, we fail to be the force majeure of our destiny. Instead, we become spectators wherein we glide from scene to scene, month to month and year to year. Instead of watching and waiting, force yourself to appreciate that you have been given a divine assignment to make our world better for the next generation. Whether or not you successfully fulfill your mission will be based on if you're guided by ego or God's whispers.

In listening to your ego that has been shaped by other people's truths, experiences, and misperceptions, you will fall short of becoming the fullness of your wholeness. You see, no one can empower you to be greater than them, nor do they always want you to be. However, when we listen to the inner victim, aka our Inner Me, we often lose ourselves because our vision becomes clouded by self-hatred, self-doubt, and self-defeat. You stop loving who you are and start coveting other people. You stop seeking to become the fullness of who God says you are by burying your wants, needs, hopes, and dreams into the shadow of another person's experiences, which causes you to die before your time. But when the soul grows weary of the things of this world, the knowledge of this world, and the people of this world, it will seek to know more. As you continually seek, know, ask, and interrogate what is perceived as truth, the truth will make you free. You will become free of the false evidence appearing real; you will become free of societal mores and free of the pretenses of man that held you. Eventually, you will discover the lover of your soul and the Creator of your heart that molded and shaped you on purpose for a life of purpose. Your voice becomes clear; your judgment is sound; your passion is contagious, and you are inspired to have, do, and be more.

I have tried to help others recreate their life story that makes their heart skip a beat and allows their spirit to be free. My mother was my first test case as I tried in vain to help her appreciate that she could use her personal strengths, investigative skills, and natural abilities to help herself and us live better lives. However, my mother was never receptive to the self-motivated younger version of herself telling her that she had it within her to uplevel her life experiences. I tried with a few of my sisters, as well. But I always felt that I failed because, in the end, they got stuck and died before their time. But perhaps, hopefully, I can ignite the brilliance within you so that you maximize your fullest potential.

You are a walking, talking, living, breathing miracle-worker manifested who has everything you need to manifest what God spoke over you. Your purpose is not to continually do the same ole, whether consciously or subconsciously, as your parents, grandparents, and ancestors have done. Nor are you here to parrot, imitate, or acquiesce to individuals who think of themselves as being worthier than you. You are here for one reason and one reason alone, which is to push against the status quo to maximize our collective success. I know it's probably hard to fully appreciate that your heart, mind, life, presence, and brilliance matters because of what you've done before you got here. But it's what you decide to do with your mind, body, soul, spirit, and business that will help you maximize your potential.

Each role you emerge into allows you to appreciate who you are and what you can do. As you know more and appreciate more, you begin to seek more, which helps us step into places we have never been before. As long as you are willing to seek more to know more, you will become empowered to do more. As you do more, you discover more of what's buried deep down on the inside of you. But if you don't allow yourself to try to change your reality, you will never unlock the brilliance within you that allows you to maximize your potential. The discovery of your brilliance empowers you to live a meaningful life that rejuvenates your soul. Once you are committed to becoming more of who God created you to be, another's judgment doesn't matter, another's deception doesn't matter, another's rejection doesn't matter, another's deceit doesn't matter, and another's harsh words don't matter. Instead, you become open to the possibility that your eyes may not have seen it all, and your ears may not have heard all of those good things God has in store for you.

Even when others are willing to wait, be still, and be complacent in their circumstance, you have an inner desire to press forward to the rhythmic cadence of your beating heart. Your soul will never be persuaded to watch and wait for someone to awaken the possibilities within you again. Whatever you do, don't get stuck in your circumstances. Don't stop dreaming. And don't stop allowing yourself to turn your vision into goals and your dreams into reality. Don't fail yourself by diminishing your mind, ignoring the tug in your heart, or negating your vision. Be, have, and do better.

Let Go and Let God

There comes a time in our lives when we find ourselves wondering how we got here, why we continually do what we do, or how we can start over. I know what it's like to live in fear of getting into yet another bad situation. Whether getting a butt whooping, getting ejected from a circle of influencers, or getting a phone call that ruins everything, I found myself in a constant, never-ending cycle of operating in fear of getting ejected.

Many have fallen because the wounds they suffered became too much to bear. This may be due to parental lies, unfulfilled dreams, or paths taken that redirected them to detours that led to nowhere. Others stopped trying to make their dreams possible when life got too hard or when they found a comfortable place that they could live in. But then there are a few who shook off the pain, threw scriptures at fear, negated the negativity, and forced themselves to believe more was possible. I have fallen, gotten stuck, and later picked myself up by pretending I was worthy of more until I activated something within me that unleashed my possibilities. I kept trying to be better, speak better, and show up better. I was driven not to be the foster kid of success.

But the very thing I didn't want to be, I found myself becoming. I knew I wanted to be successful, but I wasn't definitive. I didn't know where I was going. I didn't know where I wanted to go. But I knew I didn't want to go back to the urban hood I came from. So, I did what I learned to do, which was complain about what I didn't have. A few times, I raised my hand to volunteer to help women and kids live better than I learned to live. But maybe because my walk, my talk, my look, and my unwillingness to be controlled made people reject me. Or at least that was their excuse.

People always ask when did I become intentional about living my best life. What I realize is that I had experienced a series of moments when I was given chance after chance to uplevel my life experiences and circumstances. As a teen, when I went to Milton Hershey School, I had to level up my mindset so I didn't get kicked out of the school I had begged to stay in. At the University of Pennsylvania, I had to uplevel from being a person who always got A's for just showing up to a person who was intentional about manifesting success. If we are keeping it real, I needed to uplevel my dating life because I was kissing on too many pawns, hoping and praying they would be the kings I needed them to be to rescue me.

Every time I watched and waited, I always came up short.

I eventually realized life is not about making much about what we don't have, but making the most out of what we do have. Similar to the fairytales that I consumed to escape my traumatic realities, our quest begins with a question of whether we want to stay where we are or whether we want to seek better and pursue more. When you realize you were created on purpose for a divine purpose, you allow yourself to seek more. There is no specific time in our lives when our purpose manifests, but it often ensues upon a traumatic event. In many instances, the pain we suffered in our pasts manifests as purpose—whether the death of a loved one, loss of a job you took for granted for a long time, or escaping near death. Once you take advantage of an opportunity to make better decisions, you seek greater knowledge and understanding of how to live more and love more.

Throughout this discovery phase, you start appreciating the little things in life that you had little time to appreciate before. The added bonus is you get new days, new opportunities, and lessons learned from past missteps that brought you closer to a mission to help, love, and connect with others. When life gets bad with the unexpected ups and downs, it's better to withstand the circumstance when you push through the pain. While you are pushing through, you give yourself an opportunity to get into the movement. You don't want to be so weak that you don't move. You must fully appreciate that God is your present help. You must appreciate that the move of God is on the way, but you must continually move.

Whatever you are going through, never forget that it is not new to God. Just as He has helped you withstand the circumstances, endure worse, and overcome what others could not, He will continually uphold you, think of you, and make a way out of no way for you. Even if your new problem, new distress, and new leak in your foundation are threatening to drown you, go through the storms of life fully expecting to speak to the storms. How you perceive the problem is how you withstand the pain. If you see the situation as a curse, you will suffer more than necessary because of the emotional baggage that comes with curses. However, if you see life experiences and situations as a test of your faith, you will push through the obstacle.

If you see your abuser as merely a bad character in your story, then you will find a way to erase, replace, or remove them. And if you see life as a marathon wherein you must go through the liars, tigers, bears, abusers, deceivers, and manipulators, then you won't stay stuck in the chapters that aren't meant to kill you. Nor will you allow previous trials and tribulations to hurt your ability to manifest greater through you. The biggest secret to achieving, receiving, and becoming more than you've ever seen or heard before is to appreciate that people only understand from their perception. You will waste time, money, patience, strength, and everything important to you if you continually surround yourself with people who only do what they know. But if you want more, you must seek to know more, be around more, and understand that everyone is not on your level. Nor will they go with you when you progress from one level to the next.

No shade, but if they aren't trying to come up, then you must protect yourself and rise above the pushback, negativity and judgment to go higher than you've ever been before. No matter where you come from, who won't support you, who talks about you, or who will never make room for you, you must prove for yourself that more is possible. While that is easier said than done because of societal norms, mores, life experiences, and miseducation, you must not confirm that you conformed to everyone. Instead, you must be unapologetic in upleveling your thoughts, beliefs, actions, and habitudes. What I know for sure is our mindset matters. Unfortunately, in church, we talk more about what the devil did, the ills of society, and what NOT to wear/do more than what God has given us the power to name, claim, and achieve. If you have faith, knowledge, and appreciate who you are, you have what you need to change your fate and fulfill a greater destiny. The trick to overcome negative thinking is to shift your thoughts from where you are to where you believe you're divinely appointed to be.

More specifically, instead of holding your hand out to receive, start stretching it out to seize. Instead of wondering if you're meant to go, start asking God to lead you where you're supposed to be. Instead of using your voice to ask for permission, start speaking about what you need to do and what you feel in your spirit that God commissioned. And instead of wondering if God hears your prayers, start living by faith as though He heard and is willing to give you more. What I know for sure, the secret to becoming unstoppable is to stop stopping yourself!

Live Your Best Life

You were fearfully and wonderfully made to be who God created you to be. Whether you are religious or not, there is a universal understanding that we were created to be more than we are. For many, including myself, there is a God of all the universe who pervades our daily living to inspire, encourage, motivate, and empower each of us to be who we are. Within each moment of every day, there is a whisper, a pull in another direction, a tug at the heart that causes you to appreciate that more is possible, that love can happen, and that we can be better than our eyes have ever seen or ears have ever heard. Some people think of it as a coincidence, but the coincidence is a random act without reason. Your life, dreams, blessings, miracles, resources, and opportunities will be delayed until you fully appreciate that you are meant for more.

While the past may have disappeared, it will never be forgotten since it left a stench that serves as a constant reminder of empty promises and nightmares that keep most from dreaming dreams of building lives we love with grace and ease. But if you allow yourself to continually stay stuck in the past of not doing, having, or receiving because of the hatred and isms of others, you will continually get the same results. At the end of your day, you want to be triumphant and be confident that the life you build is the life you love and that you become who God created you to be. Accordingly, you must not only submit to the process but step into the position to make your life matter. The only way to do that is to fully appreciate that you have what it takes to rise up, step up, and uplevel your success with grace and ease.

If you want to be happy and live the life of your dreams, you must find a way to appreciate that the life you live is based on your actions, inactions, reactions, and responses. Throughout my talks and coaching sessions, people often tell me why they haven't or can't get over the pain of sexual abuse, mental abuse, discrimination, and racism. Some even email me about the trauma of not having, not knowing, and not becoming because of what happened in their past. After hugging some and touching and agreeing with others, I look them squarely in their eyes and ask them whether or not they are okay with being a whiner throughout their life or if they truly what to win. While I empathize with them, I know I only have a few moments to awaken them from their spiritual slumber. So, I do whatever it takes to jolt them awake in hopes that their response will activate their brilliance.

Through no fault of our own, our perception of truth was

passed down and force-fed to us by individuals who learned to do but never to become the fullest expression of themselves. I recall my biological mother once told me that I would end up in the same projects we lived in with a bunch of kids by different daddies. Instead of following my mother's footsteps, I made a radical decision to design the life I loved. In doing so, I positioned myself to go beyond my zip code. I gave myself permission to network in circles that didn't exist in my neighborhood. I allowed myself to believe that more was possible. I allowed myself to redesign the lines of my possibility. And I did whatever I needed to do to change the narrative that limited my potential.

Unfortunately, most people don't do what they need to do to become radically different than the environment where they grew up. Even statistics substantiate the stories we tell ourselves—what we can't do based on what others won't do. In fact, according to the Center for Disease Control and Prevention, neglect, physical abuse, custodial interference, and sexual abuse are types of child maltreatment that can lead to poor physical and mental health well into adulthood. Very few parents cultivate their children to be bold and brilliant enough to make life beautiful based on their DNA (desires, needs, and abilities). Instead, generation after generation is taught how to deal with the lies of life by getting educated, getting a job (career or spouse), and being content with what life offers. In effect, we cultivate our ego more than our essence and thus live our lives unconsciously controlling, altering, and deleting our infinite possibilities of fulfilling a greater destiny.

As children, we got away with blaming others for not

giving us what we needed to discover our strengths, weaknesses, abilities, and gifts. But there comes a time in our life when we must stop playing the blame game and take responsibility for outcomes. We must pick up our own mats. We must give ourselves permission to live beyond our life experiences and circumstances. We must nurture ourselves. We must invest in the hopes, prayers, dreams, and miracles our ancestors could have ever imagined. And we must stand in our power to become the fullness of who we are. Own your power to speak what you seek. You must own your power to turn curses into blessings. You must own your power to stop sabotaging yourself with shoulda, woulda, and coulda. You must also own your power to become the fearfully and wonderfully made woman God created you to be.

Much like Elizabeth, Ruth, Mary, and Zelophehad's five daughters in the Bible, you must own your power to evolve into who you need to be to manifest a greater destiny. You must never allow what others didn't do or won't do to keep you from achieving what's meant for you. Never allow anyone to make you feel worthless. Instead, do whatever good work you need to build yourself up. Some will like you, others will use you, and others will tolerate you. However, only you can motivate yourself to do whatever it takes to become a better version of yourself. Similarly, stop punishing yourself for what you did in the past because you can't have a prosperous future if you have a prodigal mindset.

As you continually stand in your power to live, love, and lead a greater destiny, you will fully appreciate the power of God—the spark of God, if you will—that helps you change the trajectory of your destiny. Find a way to actualize what you visualize to make your vision matter. Be the hearer of God's whispers that helps you move out of your own way. Be the doer of God's Word so you can implement newfound lessons to manifest greater blessings. Be the one who operates in spirit and in truth to manifest every good thing God spoke over you. As you find what you need to overcome the little things in life, you will discover the power to achieve, receive, and become what God spoke over you before he breathed goodness and greatness into you.

Pursue Your Purpose

Have you ever found yourself in a place that didn't feel right? In that place, you tried to look the part, dress the part, and show up for the part, but for some reason your enough wasn't good enough? I can't remember when I stopped trying to be a better version of myself—for others. I tried to be the best girlfriend to the wrong man. I tried to be the best lawyer for the wrong clients. I tried to be the best daughter to someone who couldn't appreciate my existence. For many years, I sat, stumbled, and benched myself because I didn't like my walk, my talk, and the essence of who I was based on the success of another. The worst thing I ever did in my path to success was compare my voice, vision, and value to other people. I wanted what other people had so much that I tried to get in and fit in where I wasn't created to belong.

TONI MOORE ESQ.

It is natural to fear what we don't know because we were taught from birth to avoid what we don't know, and we were taught other people's fears, failures, and limitations from our parents, caretakers, teachers, and friends. It's a rare find to be exposed to another's truth and not be infected or affected by it. But it is a blessing to appreciate that God prepared each of us with unique resources to be of service to someone. Just as God prepared different birds and fish of the sea, He made us different on purpose. He made some hearers, some doers, some seekers, some explorers, some to serve, and still, others to be heard. No two messages are the same, just as no two messengers are the message based on choices made throughout their life experience. For more years than I can remember, I always wanted to be smarter, prettier, cuter, richer, and more talented, much like the archetype of the perfect girls. I almost gave up on myself because every time I tried to take two steps forward, I found myself living in a space and place that resembled more of my beginnings.

After scratching and surviving and trying to get in where I thought I could fit in, I got tired of living the life I had created. I was confused about the emptiness I felt since I had done everything I thought successful people did. I went to school, got good grades, got a job, got married, lived in a progressive neighborhood, and connected with the right organizations. I never knew how to do anything more than what was needed to get by. And despite learning from an early age to sit still, be polite, and keep my mouth shut, knowing and saying what I wanted to say wasn't difficult either. I so wanted to be the elusive perfect, powerful, and popular girl everyone seemed to like. What I never appreciated is that the elusive perfect girl is comfortable in her own skin.

I would have been further along on my life journey if I would have done what I needed to do to uplevel in every aspect of my life. But none of us can change the past. If we could, more than likely we wouldn't be who we needed to become. I tried to pretend that I didn't know the pain of an extension cord. I tried to pretend that the person I broke bread with didn't molest me. I tried to pretend that my heartbreak of not having and not being didn't hurt more than the man I loved leaving me because he was an empty shell of himself. God has a way of showing us our potential so that we pursue our purpose—even if we must go through the storms, setbacks, negativities, and series of defeats.

Your life is a testament of your beliefs. No one on this earth can help you be who God created you to be other than you. From the beginning to the end, you have been given trials, tribulations, and lessons that were not meant to break you but help you appreciate what God put in you. Similarly, each day offers new blessings, mercies, and opportunities to give you hope that something more is in store. Regardless of what your eyes see, follow your heart, because your heart serves as a homing device that leads you to the path that was created by your maker. While seeking and processing towards this path, you will discover the pathway to success that pushes you to the front of the room. You will also find the strength to overcome the obstacle that helps you make more of your dreams possible. What is often not mentioned yet must be understood is that our lives may not be our own, but we must own it. We must make our dreams, life vision, and goals a priority. If we don't own our power, we will fail ourselves, our

Divine mission, and our legacy.

Believe me when I say upleveling your mind, body, and spirit to purposefully align to the Divine is hard. However, living in regret is harder. Living beneath one's Godly privileges is hard, and having a dream but not living the dream is hard. As eternal spirits journeying through this finite life, you must own your power to become a beacon of hope. You must own your power to write a formula for your success. You must find a way to bridge the gap between your destiny and reality. You must position yourself to become the fullest expression of yourself. You must own the power that helps you walk right, talk right, and want to live beyond what's insight. To make the impossible possible, you must commit to seeking and seizing more than ever before.

Never decrease your standards for anything or anyone. You are a queen who is worthy of love, respect, peace, joy, and happiness. The things you most want are not given but revealed, claimed, and protected moment by moment, day by day. Unfortunately, a scarcity mindset will never allow you to live your best life. Similarly, asking permission to live on purpose will keep you stuck. Watching and waiting for the perfect person, place, and/or thing will keep you tethered to the places and spaces you were born to overcome. In contrast, when you anchor your beliefs to become the blessed version of yourself, you get a chance to continually ignite your spirit and set your soul free to align with the Divine and unleash your possibilities.

Whatever you want for tomorrow, you must become skillful at molding and shaping what comes your way today. Unfortunately, if you continually do what you've always done, you will get the same results. If you don't like who you are, where you are, or the life you are currently living, you must find the power within you to make a difference for yourself. While it may appear comfortable to watch, wait, and wish inside your self-made cocoon, you must eventually come to live a life that is meaningful to you. Now whether you get asked out, pushed out, snatched, or drawn-out is based on your decisions, responses, and reactions to what comes your way. But if you allow yourself to be still for a moment, you can get very specific about how you want to live. You can reframe your destiny by speaking blessings over your life. Never forget freewill is a blessing. You can use it for good. You can choose differently. You can even force yourself to turn dreams into reality by focusing your time, energy and money into completing one task at a time. So, determine how you want to live and what you are willing to do to achieve it. Be willing to commit to living the life you love regardless of or how you are forced to live your life throughout the in-between.

Unleash Your Greatness

There comes a time in everyone's life that we experience loss. Whether it's the loss of a loved one, money, or job, the loss is significant, and it causes our souls to weep. In effect, we find ourselves repeatedly singing the blues of doom and gloom. But you are not meant to sing the blues for the rest of your life. God offers new mercies, blessings, and opportunities to sing a new song. Regardless of what you've experienced, don't allow it to define you, bind you, or blind you to your endless possibilities. Similarly, don't allow doom and gloom to keep your thoughts anchored to darkness, negativity, and defeat. Unfortunately, if you have repeatedly allowed yourself to go into a spiritual depression about what happened in the past, you will miss out on fulfilling a greater destiny. But when you find a way to push past the brokenness, you will appreciate the rest of what was prepared for you.

We've lived in the darkness long enough. We are meant to seek, know, and walk in the light that is brighter than we've ever seen before. Don't dimmer your shine, lose hope, or stop asking for better. Keep demanding larger slices of the proverbial pie so you don't miss out. My mom was a God-fearing woman, but after one too many missiles, miscreants, and mishaps, she missed out on using her Divine power to design a life she deserved and desired. Unfortunately, instead of resolving the issues and conflict from a place of power, she placated her emotions by creating happiness outside of herself. She went to conferences, revivals, and her family to get recharged. In so doing, she allowed the poison of regret and frustration to grow as a spiritual wound that festered in her mind, body, and spirit instead of working out her own salvation. By the time my mother reached forty, she had stopped running, stopped fighting, and stopped trying to live the life she desired.

After experiencing one too many trials, devastations, disappointments and heartbreaks, Momma became so emotionally bankrupt that she no longer had the energy to restore herself from the inside out. In many ways, my life paralleled my mother's. For many years, I tried running away from the very thing I felt—a life of guilt, repentance, and penitence. But I had no vision, no plans, and no strategies about where I was going. Similar to broken records, you will need to do something to move the needle. If you need to talk with a counselor, do it. If you need to meet with a support group, do it. If you need to speak uplifting scriptures or affirmations every day, do it. Even if you need to pray every day for God to help you open your eyes to your fullest potential, do it. Instead of having a "woe is me" or "why me" mentality, you should have an "I can have it all, do it all, and achieve it all" mentality.

In effect, you will appreciate that opportunities are often hidden on roads less traveled, embodied in burdens, and hidden amongst the thorny garden of obstacles. Just know if you believe you are blessed and highly favored, your lifestyle changes. You won't have an insatiable need to get in where you seemingly don't fit in or try to be loved by anybody and everybody in hopes of finding meaning. Instead, you will continually make decisions about who you are and what you want. Additionally, you will have the boldness to set standards, boundaries, and priorities to nurture and protect what you hold dear, such as peace, joy, love, and a desire to become better. In effect, you will eat better, look better, walk better, and think better about your ability to make your hopes and dreams come true.

In the meantime, imagine your life beyond the issue that keeps you stuck. Imagine what you are doing, saying, and achieving. What does that look like to you? Make it real by feeling the experience in your mind. Now that you placed a new image in your mind, create a plan to manifest it for you. By making a new image in your mind based on what your heart desires, you make room for more. And if you bring faith into the mix, God will provide the substance for the very things you hope for. God will even create in your heart a new song that restores, inspires, and motivates you to appreciate that you are meant for more. Never forget that thoughts are things, and as the master of your mind, you can change your world by singing a new song of joy, happiness, and success.

You are also the author and finisher of your fate based on your faith. The mere act of asking helps a person receive what they need because words change worlds. When you speak negativity, you receive negativity because energy goes where you allow your words to flow. In contrast, when you speak positivity, you attract positivity to ensure your words don't return void. Similarly, as you speak abundance, you will appreciate more opportunities to ensure you achieve abundance. I truly believe each of us has a voice of reason that helped us throughout our lives to seek better and press for more. Unfortunately, we fail to listen to it; we drown it out with substances, negativity, television, and/or another's truth. However, when we allow ourselves to appreciate that our voice, our words, and our thoughts matter, we eventually discover the still, quiet voice of God. Once you discover the Voice, you will find that God has been leading, directing, and empowering you to let go, move on, and keep pressing for more.

While there is no secret to what God can do, the key to achieving something is believing that anything is possible. Just know what God once did for others, He is more than willing, ready, and able to do the same for you. However, in order to achieve more, you must ask, seek, and constantly walk in victory to seize what you need within each moment of every day. Don't try to get in or fit in where you don't belong. Free yourself to align with the Divine so that you don't limit yourself. Be bold in embracing who God created you to be. Free yourself to become who God created you to be. While our differences may cause problems, trauma, and drama, appreciating them is the very thing that will help you fulfill a greater destiny.

Unfortunately, when I looked back over my life, I didn't like it. Worse yet, the people I had tried to please didn't appreciate it but instead expected more of me. It wasn't until I took my complaints to the heavens about the state of my world that I began to realize I allowed myself to be conformed by things of this world. I started asking God to help me become a better version of myself, and that's when my life began to change. It wasn't sudden or automatic, but I started to see where I could make changes, and they were received. Then I began to have the boldness to set boundaries, which helped me appreciate that I was more than enough to design a life that I loved. But when my life became better, I realized my better was based on the little I asked for instead of the more that was already mine. In effect, I started seeking better, pursuing greater, and doing more of the things that mattered most to me, like appreciating the voice of acceptance.

While I lost some friends and was rejected by others for the first time in a long time, I actually liked the reflection in my mirror. I even started to turn the mirror on my legal clients so they, too, could change their words to change their worlds. Then the biggest trial came when someone who thought she was dying reached out to me. I didn't think I was worthy because in church only licensed individuals were permitted to speak God's truth. But the woman dying in the hospital room wanted to speak to me, and I couldn't say no because in many ways, she reminded me of myself when I was down on my knees desperately pleading for someone to find a way to love me. Somehow helping her helped me awaken my spirit from my slumber.

My awakening came in enough time for me to discover that I didn't want to walk away from my husband. I awakened in enough time to fuel my faith to get through my season of infertility. Once I went through that season, I found a way to manifest a fulfilling life outside of the endless cycle of billable hours so much so that I ran a charitable organization for women and girls. I later conjured up enough love to stop suffering in my life and start succeeding throughout my life. I was able to defy my realities because I stopped waiting for someone to rescue me. I didn't want to be remembered as the woman who ALMOST accomplished something. I spoke up to the heavens so that I could change my fate.

I now find opportunities to awaken others by challenging women to redefine their life experiences. I take every opportunity to ask women to think about the big picture, the final outcome, and ultimate experience. After living the life I've lived, I try to motivate others to shift their focus from the huge demands to the mini goals. You must obsess more about the benefits than the burdens. You must ignore the price of the oil and press for the prize of obtaining it. You must become obsessed with having, doing, achieving, and manifesting greater success on this side of heaven.

Master Your Pieces

Many women find themselves trying to fabricate a fairytale from life experiences and circumstances they fell into. Some women grow up believing they were given life to be objectified as a man's doormat instead of being glorified as his helpmeet. Other women grow up to believe love is a battlefield in that they must lie, deceive, and scratch and survive throughout life in hopes of getting a few crumbs and a few steps ahead of the generations before them. And still, another group of women who love God and praise God don't trust God enough to help them live a better life. In effect, most women are not satisfied with the life they live, nor do they know how to live the life they're given. Instead, they watch and wait on a touch, a word, or someone to help them live a better life.

In so many ways, I could have been an almost type of woman. I almost became a private school reject, almost became a college flunk out, almost became a drug dealer's mule, and almost became a young man's baby mother because I truly thought I could matter to someone who didn't matter to himself. But God had purposed and planned that I become a trailblazer. Thankfully, something within me wouldn't allow me to stop where other people stopped. Even when I was alone and by myself, my spirit reminded me of my dreams of living a dream life where I didn't have to tiptoe around judgmental people or fear being tossed from a tribe I wasn't born into.

As a self-help junkie who was obsessed with Greek mythology, fairytales, and fantasy, I knew I could be better because God allowed others who had humble beginnings similar to my own to live better lives and fulfill greater legacies. However, my spirit knew mere self-help wouldn't work because I couldn't help myself emerge as the fearfully and wonderfully made woman God created me to be. I didn't want to just survive life but thrive in it. Besides, I didn't want to live with barely enough, but I wanted to find a way to live my dreams. At school, I read about women who met their Prince Charming and lived happily ever after. At church, I learned about the life we would live in heaven. Eventually, I got sick and tired of being sick and tired of being on the endless cycle of ducking, dodging, or surviving a seeming stronghold that kept me close to the very things that I was running from. So, I forced myself to uplevel.

Truth be told, I stumbled into various aspects of the broke woman—uncomfortable, unworthy, and waiting to exhale. While waiting for my Savior, Fairy Godmother, and Prince

Charming, I realized I would live a whole life waiting for others only to die full of hopes and dreams. I even tried to get in and fit in the places and spaces in hopes that someone would validate my existence. I thought degrees and certifications would fill the emptiness in me, but none did. I thought attending a very popular church would help me expand into my enoughness. Instead, I found myself diminishing my presence because my lack was emphasized more than my possibilities. Even the professional setting was bizarre because I didn't have a sponsor or mentor to help me walk through the labyrinth of success.

After making many mistakes and missteps, I eventually realized that life is not about what we don't have, but making the most out of what we do have. Similar to the fairytales that I consumed to escape my traumatic realities, our quest begins with a question of whether we want to stay where we are or seek better and pursue more. What I failed to appreciate until many years later is that what was most attractive about the seemingly perfect girl was that she was comfortable in her own skin. In fact, most men and women I was most attracted to were the ones who were unapologetic about who they were, how they looked, and how they showed up in their world. They just put themselves together, sang their song, created their business, used their words, and showed up as the full epitome of who they decided they would be.

It took me a long time to realize the vision I had for my life would never become my reality until I made living it a priority. After I graduated from college and later law school, I got married, got a job, and started expecting others to help me, guide me, and promote me to the next level—almost like school. But no one did. When I finally decided to do something for myself, I kept making mistakes because I didn't know anyone who was trying to uplevel their success beyond their socioeconomic class passionately, purposefully, and powerfully. Instead, most of the people I asked discouraged me instead of encouraging me to live beyond their reality. So, I toned down on sharing my dreams and eventually sacrificed my dreams so I could survive my reality. This almost worked until I became sick and tired of working long days, having little to no time with my children, hoping and wanting more but only living a few hours a week on the weekend. I was so desperate for something more that I stumbled along my yellow brick road experience.

Similarly, when you're in situations in life wherein you are dimming your shine to survive, you must assess yourself. You must determine if what you're doing will keep you broke, busted, and disgusted, or if it will empower you to uplevel into a better version of yourself. You're not meant to fit into spaces and places where you don't belong. Nor are you just meant to survive life. In fact, you're meant to thrive in your life so that you grow into the fullest version of yourself. Take a moment to appreciate that you have what it takes to be successful. You don't always have to survive. You don't even have to get by. Nor do you need to deny yourself of your desires. You only need to give yourself permission to prosper above and beyond your life experiences and circumstances.

In giving myself permission to become the best version of myself, I stopped wondering if I was smart enough, pretty enough, skinny enough, or confident enough to present myself as an option. After I learned that my dad wasn't my real dad,

114

and that some of my family demonized me for daring to ask about my biological connections, I realized those who tried to demonize me were not free themselves. Half of them didn't even like themselves enough to present the fullness of who they are to the world. And the other group of people who thought I became too much to handle, disrespected the presence of God in me. While we cannot choose our Once Upon a Time, we are given opportunity after opportunity to manifest a happier ever after. In every story, there is a beginning, middle, and end, but in life, nothing is promised, nor is anything guaranteed. Everything we do in the middle can help us change the end of each verse and chapter that will lead, guide, and motivate us to recreate a better ending. So, if you take a leap of faith and end up in the wrong job, you don't have to stay there. If you chase after a lover who ends up being a nightmare, you don't have to stay with them. Even if you start a business and end up almost bankrupting yourself two, three, six times, you can always give yourself a restart blessing.

You must give yourself permission to live a life that is beautiful to you. Whether by word, action, or deed, you get to choose what is next for you. Don't seek validation for achieving yet another milestone in life. If you felt in your spirit that God called you to have more, do more, and be more, then do it. Command your faith to pursue what was laid upon your heart. Similarly, if you feel you are supposed to turn your trauma into a triumphant story by changing your thoughts, actions, and words, then do it. As long as you wait for another's permission and/or acceptance, you make their voice and vision bigger than God's whispers. Similarly, don't wait for the perfect man, perfect plan, or perfect time to take a leap of faith. God is your present help in your time of need. Once you feel within your knower that it is time for you to become better in life and business, you must move out of your way and just be who you believe you were created to be by the Most-High God. What I've learned from many trials and tribulations is that no one could do for me what I needed to do for myself. God planned and purposed for you to be successful based on your gifts, wisdom, talent, knowledge, skills, and abilities. So, don't waste your greatness. Do more with it.

Find Your Path

A person's self-defining moment is when they finally realize that the pain of their past was part of the process of becoming who they needed to be to bless and encourage someone else. As long as we hold on to the pain, we will continually limit ourselves from being the person we need to be. We will stumble, fall down, crawl back up, and when the going gets really tough, stay down. But what I know for sure, in every story, there is a beginning, middle, and end. Unfortunately, if we hold onto everything that happens to us, we will miss out on helping ourselves get out of the losing phase of life. If we get so fixated on how we messed up, we will also miss out on learning the lesson that helps us get to our next phase.

For most of my life, I have always wondered how some

people are more successful at living their blessed life while others scratch and survive throughout their life. Oftentimes, both have the same educational and socio-economical background. Yet, one lives the life they live, and the other always gives it. We're all born of purpose. Within us, there is something that shines, resonates, responds, and rejoices when we hear something that moves us from inactivity to implementation. But our divine purpose is not to continually do the same old same, nor is it to try to get in to fit in, nor is it to try to appease everybody. The best thing you can do for yourself is to love yourself enough to rewrite your story so that you can become the woman of your dreams. Transforming your mindset so you become who you're born to be is easier to say but actually harder to do. Trials, tribulations, and spiritual warfare is real. Don't placate your emotions or patch up the pain by making yourself busy creating happiness outside of yourself. The poison of regret and frustration will just gnaw at your soul so much so that your spiritual wounds became a sceptic. The poison infects your mind, body, and spirit. I've been there, done that—twice—once through my mother's life's circumstance and through my own experiences.

By the time my mother reached thirty years of age, she had stopped running, stopped fighting, and stopped trying to live the life she desired. Instead, after experiencing one too many devastations, disappointments, and heartbreaks, she became so emotionally bankrupt that she no longer had the energy to restore herself from the inside out. When I graduated from the University of Pennsylvania, I set my eyes on law school. Once I graduated from law school, I started out as a law clerk, skipping through serving as a commercial litigator, and became fixated on helping others legally get through their traumatic life experiences. I sacrificed my time, dreams, passion, and skills to help others. Unfortunately, despite accumulating degrees, helping others, and living on the other side of the street, I realized that much like Momma, I was not living my best life. I was no longer demanding the larger slice of the figurative pie.

Every time I tried to take two steps forward, I found myself living in a space and place that resembled more of my beginnings. After scratching, surviving, and trying to get in where I thought I could fit in, I got tired of living the life I had created. I never knew how to do anything more than what was needed to scratch, survive, and get by. Even when I became a lawyer, advocating for others to get what they deserved or pleading to my clients not to give up on their destiny, I found myself crying in my pillow because the life I lived didn't reflect what I had hoped to see. Sadly, when I complained, some people demonized me for not being satisfied with what I had. Others quoted scriptures and told me to pray but never gave me guidance on how, why, and what to do when my feelings overshadowed my faith. And others totally ignored me because they had not experienced what I was complaining about.

Much like Eve in the Bible, I always wanted pleasure in life. So, I tried to take shortcuts to get what I wanted, which resulted in the cycle of rejection, pain, sorrow, frustration, and embarrassment. Ever since I can remember, I reached for what appeared wonderful for a lifetime only to undergo the painful process over and over again. Eventually, the pain of not knowing fed my fears, which caused me to stop doing and

119

ultimately stop being wonderful enough to wander, seek, know, and do to become who I was born to be. However, after years of not doing, I became bitter and frustrated about not having the freedom to be myself. Even as a grown woman, I found myself complaining about what people wouldn't do or allow me to do to the point that I became so frustrated that my spirit started praying for me, which eventually stirred my soul awake.

When I was at my worst, God helped me appreciate that we are not meant to live in regret, but to appreciate that some things happen because of choices we made. Maybe we didn't know, wasn't taught, or tried to experiment with life on our own terms because we were not taught better. Still, ultimately, we have a choice of whether or not we will continually live the life that's been thrown at us or if we will allow ourselves to seek to know more, do more, and/or be more. After several serial mistakes, missteps, mistreatments, and misunderstandings, I finally learned that life was a journey and that I was the co-creator of my life story. So, instead of giving everything I had in hopes of pleasing all or trying to get in where I thought I should fit in, I sought within myself to seek, know, and ask God of my soul's purpose. That's when I discovered I was more than enough to manifest and live a life I not only loved but that I could thrive in.

Once my spirit was activated, and my soul became attracted to the possibilities of living bigger, better, and bolder, I started to become curious again. I started thinking again, imagining again, and believing in myself again. The thought in itself was radical because I come from a long line of people who believed that life only happened as a result of agreeing, asking for permission, and receiving confirmation. However, after years of hoping, dreaming, and not doing, I began to seek to know more about the trailblazers, spiritualists, and those who made radical shifts in their lives, which ultimately led me to discover God who loves me, knows me, and empowers me to be a better version of myself no matter what.

You were fearfully and wonderfully made by an all-knowing, all-seeing, and all-powerful God to be who you are. Based on your life experiences, circumstances, and realities, you either hear the fearful or the wonderful since we are motivated by either pain or pleasure. God planned and purposed for you to prosper before anyone had an opinion of you. Moreover, each of us has a path that God designed for us to prosper in. So, you need to identify what works for you. Find your sweet spot. Find the thing that helps you appreciate the passage we call life. Find the thing that gives you meaning for being. While God's grace is sufficient, you must not allow the wounds to become your tombs. You must not allow the miseducation to keep you from elevating. You must not allow yourself to be complacent in the Sea of Sameness. Seek greater within you. Change your narrative so you can uplevel in everything. You need to fully appreciate that you are in this world for a reason. Seek the reason, be the reason, be the solution, and be the answer. Just don't get stuck and stay where you are. Don't just watch for more; work out your own salvation until you manifest overflow. Don't just hope and pray someone will help you prevail. You must take up your own mat, understand that your mindset matters, and work out your own soul's salvation with fear that God will get you if you don't become the best version of yourself.

Through the years, wisdom has taught me that life is like a constant treasure hunt in that we have a beautiful, yet challenging journey. Whether we must conquer our fears, push back negativity, or stumble in the dark in hopes of solving some puzzle, we must do whatever it takes to uplevel our legacy. Many have spent their entire life seeking the ultimate answer to unlocking the infinite mysteries presented to us by life. Some have been satisfied with only merely looking upward instead of up, down, and all around to appreciate the treasures life offers. Others have been satisfied with the collectibles life offers, such as money, power, respect, degrees, expensive cars, and bigger houses. And still, others have taken a more philosophical approach in their search for answers to gain a better understanding of taking a shortcut to obtain their treasures.

You must seek the path that allows you to be your best self. Seek the place wherein you no longer weep or seek approval from people who dropped you off without the decency of telling you. Seek the place that fulfills you and brings you joy. Seek the place you crave so that you can live your best wherein you are needed, loved, and appreciated for who you are and all that you can do. Once you find the place, you'll discover that what you went through isn't about you. That trauma, isms, and schisms wasn't about you. But now that you went through the pain, you can help people walk through what you worked through. The solutions others need are within you. Others don't have to suffer if you share the solution. Others don't have to be stagnant if you share the solution. If you don't share the solution, those people who are attached to you will fall and falter because you failed to share what you learned to do.

You have what you need to pick yourself up, turn yourself around, and place your feet on solid ground. Don't get stuck in the realities of what happened. Focus on your next. Allow God to be your Waymaker. Let Him be your present help—your end all and be all. Let God dream and manifest through you. Allow Him to manifest more through you. Don't skate through life so you avoid the hard parts. Don't pretend that you aren't instantly triggered by the very people you are supposed to love on this side of heaven. And let's not pretend that things happen suddenly without God's interceding on your behalf. When you know what you want, you will seek the opportunity to manifest what you believe in your heart is yours. Will this be easy? No, because most of us have never been given the opportunity to step up, step out, and show up for ourselves. However, when you truly appreciate that God created a perfect path that allows you to hope, dream, flow, grow, and prosper on this side of heaven, you will stop living beneath the Divine's privileges. Instead, you will start asking, seeking, speaking, and showing up so you can have, do, and be the fullness of who you are meant to be on this side of heaven.

Own Your Power

Have you found the thing that makes you want to spread your creative wings, that brings you joy, or makes your heart sing? I thought I did, but then I stopped, found it again, then stopped because I thought it should be something else. Then I found it again. The funny thing is, it has always been the same, but my perception of it changed. Instead of complaining about what it wasn't, I began appreciating what it could be. Throughout my life, I continued to make some progress but then sabotaged my footsteps because my mind never changed even though my situation had changed dramatically! While I was no longer the traumatized little girl who had become so victimized throughout life that I wanted to die, I still possessed the victim mentality. However, when I realized my vision of love would not be manifested by anyone but me, I committed to doing whatever I needed to do to manifest success in my own special way!

I had to go deep within the depths of my soul to untether my soul to what kept me anchored in the spirit of abandonment, worthlessness, and hopelessness. When I did my inner-soul healing, I thought I needed to go to the place where the man with the big hands molested me when I was five years old. In the midst of my parents and a house full of guests, the man tickled me until I felt his stiffness and wouldn't let me off until he was soft. It was even worse when he forced me to touch and stroke his manhood at the age of ten as my older sister shopped at the grocery store. But when I learned at around thirty-nine years old that my dad wasn't my father, I realized I had to go to a younger age when someone took my voice from me. I had to go to the place in my soul wherein my four-year-old self was abandoned by my daddy, who wasn't my biological father. After I told him that Momma lied to both of us about his biological connection, he told me how he never came for me when I convinced my baby sitter to call and tell him that Momma had kidnapped me and forced me to live with her and her husband.

As I heard my Daddy's words, tears dripped absently from my eyes as my soul recalled what happened, but my ego had allowed me to forget. You see, Momma's new husband wanted all his kids' last names to match his. But at four years old, I knew who I was, and I refused to listen. So, Momma had to do what she had to do to force me to stop saying Anderson and start saying her husband's last name. While I don't remember what happened by the time I was six, I forgot calling Daddy and started shrinking from my mother and her husband. So, when the big man did what he did, and more followed him, I never told a soul because I didn't want to get in trouble. Even when I was grown and was raped on Penn State's campus three times, I didn't tell.

I had to heal myself from within by mentally walking myself to heal the spiritual wounds inflicted upon me at 4, 5, 9, 11, and 16 years of age. I needed to remind them that nothing was their fault; I wanted to ensure those wounded places knew worse would happen in my college years, but I would overcome as I pressed through. I then had to heal my self-inflicted wounds wherein I hurt myself by speaking positivity over myself. I needed to become whole in my body, mind, and soul. In so doing, I unleashed what tethered me to the pain so that I could uplevel to higher heights and deeper depths throughout life. If you're silently hurting from what happened to you, it's time to level up your mind, soul, and spirit.

While we can't change the past, we can defuse its power by addressing what happened, resolving any past issues, letting go of any remnants that affect you, and surrendering to our present moment. Just know the pain in our past will continuously invade our presence until we digest the leftovers. If you don't allow yourself to go beyond being laughed at, ridiculed, rejected, or even doubtful that you could see better days, then you won't. You will be like millions of people who get stuck in their "Once Upon a Time" story. Or what their momma did or didn't do in their story. Or even worse, what their homie, lover, and/or friend failed to do in their story. Much like a colicky child that can't be appeased or a rebellious teen that wants to be seen, pain shows up once triggered from an unmet need, expectation, or want.

TONI MOORE ESQ.

Whether consciously or subconsciously, the negativity continues because the ego it's meant to protect feeds off of it. The more negativity, the more likely a person becomes negative. Negativity attracts more negativity and thus controls you because it exudes from you. That is until something happens to jar your spirit awake, and you no longer like where you are in life or what you've become. God's greatness is much bigger than your pain, your hurts, your unmet needs, and your spiritual wounds. The greater within you is more than enough to release, repair, and restore you from the ego that keeps you stuck, stumbling, and weeping. You need only tap into it, explore the pain, and deal with what you need to heal from.

If you don't want to be stuck in the mistrust, distrust infant stage of life, you must deal with your pain. You must get to the root of who hurt you, what hurts you, and what continually hurts you. You must interrogate it; find out the message playing in the background at the subconscious level. You must find out why you are stuck at that pain point. PRESS on it to discover how it bleeds out into your life and what harm it has caused. Then you must stop the pain from keeping you from stumbling and wandering as a crippled. In so doing, you must recreate the narrative by going to the story and retelling it now that you know better. Just know, your brain doesn't fully appreciate the distinction between what actually happened and what you BELIEVE happened to you. So, take an inner journey to do an inventory of your spiritual wounds, aka your trigger zones, and restore your mind, body, and spirit.

The wholeness of who we are as multi-talented, unique, worthy, and purposeful women encompasses all aspects of our emotional being. We experience our worst days when we focus on our fears, defects, and deficiencies. We experience our best days when we feel appreciated, productive, and worthy of others' attention, time, love, acceptance, and praise. Wow, that's scary but true! Let's be honest; the pain of rejection lasts longer than what sticks and stones can ever do to your bones and can greatly impact our self-esteem unless we learn to become victors over our emotions instead of victims of them. While you have the power to speak things into existence as though they were, decreeing and declaring is not enough!

I've been there, done that, and witnessed others frustrate themselves awaiting something to happen. Writing goals and creating vision boards is not enough. Don't get me wrong, I have a vision storyboard and have helped others create their business board, book board, and financial freedom board. However, through the years of trying to step out of the sea of sameness, I've learned the importance of continual decree, declare, AND doing as though we're more than enough to live your dreams. In advocating for yourself, you will encounter enemies, and some people will reject you. However, instead of taking rejection personally, be mindful that there is a reason for each season. Some things lie dormant, while others blossom, wither away, and fall away. Similarly, some things and people come into our lives as blessings and others as lessons based on God's plans and purpose for our lives. This has never been put better than in the "Serenity Prayer" created by the theologian Reinhold Niebuhr and later adopted by Alcoholics' Anonymous: *God, grant me the serenity to accept the things I cannot change, the courage to change the things I can, and the wisdom to know the difference.* Accordingly, don't compare yourself or limit yourself based on what you see, but

129

take moments in each day to appreciate that the most beautiful things can be manifested by you. In fact, speak what you seek to become the fullest manifestation of who you are.

Speak greatness over your life and into the soil of your existence. Tell yourself that you are a beacon of light that gives others hope. You are the future millionaire that creates foundations and endowments that help others. You are a miracle worker that manifests money miracles. You are a vessel that God continually uses. You are more than enough to bless others. You are cheerfully giving unto others. You are the head and not the tail. You are the lender and not the borrower. You are the modern-day virtuous woman who unlocks, unleashes, and uses every good thing that has been stored by the Most-High God into you. If you need help, follow this pattern. You have the power to manifest greater. You will use your mouth to manifest what you want to see. You are more than a conqueror. You are a miracle worker. You have the power to be clear and concise. You are worthy of living the life you want. When you stand in the fullness of who you are, you manifest success at greater levels. So, allow yourself to be who God created you to be. Always expect goodness, mercy, and grace to follow you. Embrace the fullness of who you are, and speak blessings over your life. Despite your realities, decree and declare into the soil of your existence that your family is blessed. Your children are blessed. Your business is blessed. Your church is blessed. Your future is blessed. Your legacy is blessed. Continually decree and declare who you are and what you shall see to manifest greater things. When you want more, then ask for more, expect more, and seek more. But never decrease your standard for anything or anyone, because you are a queen who is worthy of love, respect, joy, peace, and happiness.

If love becomes a battlefield or you become frustrated about your living circumstances, then it's time to move on. Just know, the things you most want are not given but revealed, claimed, and protected moment by moment and day by day. I thought if I had the right parents, lived in the right neighborhood, had the right clothes, and became attached to the right guy, my life would somehow become meaningful—the life you love according to God's plan and purpose for you. Unfortunately, most don't get to live a life of true fulfillment wherein love, peace, and happiness is supreme. Instead, they live a life of scarcity, devastation, and negativity because they fail to appreciate that their hopes and dreams are God's way of encouraging them to seek better, pursue greater, and overcome more.

Lastly, and most importantly, the very thing you believe will make your life better is already within you but must be pulled from you by you. So, if you want to see what you've never seen before or hear what you've never heard before, you must do what you've never done before. Step out on faith for yourself. Just know, nothing changes if nothing changes, but with a little faith in God, all things are a possibility. I used to beat myself up because I only did what I knew and/or wanted to do, which stunted my growth. But despite my faults, I always appreciated there could be more. As I took steps of faith in hopes of seeing better, I started doing better, and I started appreciating that I could do more for myself. By refusing to absently take in another's negativity, I bolstered my ability to stop listening to my own critical voice of fear and doubt. Never forget that to achieve anything, you must believe in your endless possibilities. You must allow yourself to jump out of the boat, become curious beyond your comfort zone, and become a doer of your dreams. In so doing, you empower yourself to go beyond your reality. You empower yourself to develop your faith muscles, and you give yourself the opportunity to own your power and fulfill your destiny.

Shine Your Light

Did you know you are a spark of God? There is something divine deep within you that helps you see possibilities in the valleys and shadows of life, and appreciate goodness and abundance in the midst of dry bones. Similarly, the clarity of your brilliance is based on whom or what is blocking you from the Source of whom all miracles, favor, and blessings flow. You are blessed and highly favored to live your best life and manifest greater things throughout your life. In fact, God has spoken greatness over your life and given you the power to live, love, and lead a greater legacy limitlessly. There is only one of you; no one else like you came before you or will come after you. Remember that your dreams, passion, goals, plans and purpose, ideas, quirks, and desires are wrapped up within the beauty of you. So, when you come alive, the whole world benefits from your LIGHT.

We are all like diamonds in the rough. However, some get picked up quickly based on their star power, some need a little polishing based on sitting near the heat, and others show up in their own due season. Unfortunately, just like everything else in life, we compare our shine to another's shine and do whatever we can to get what they have. In effect, we go here, there, and everywhere seeking to know how we can be better, greater, and stronger but never fully appreciate the brilliance within ourselves. Instead, we allow others to take our shine, diminish our shine, block our shine, and ignore our shine so much that we forget our shine and die with our shine inside of us. Even in our businesses, we try to emulate, replicate, and duplicate another's brilliance instead of showcasing our own.

There are different facets about you, different sides to you, and different stories about you since the beginning of time. Ever since the day of your birth, you shined brightly to someone, and they saw another facet about you when they saw your comedic side or your serious side. Moreover, they even saw the very determined side of you and the side of you that couldn't be broken. Sometimes, another person in a different part of your life saw a side of you where you were jealous— the possessive side of you. Then there were some parts in your life that you'd rather not talk about, but they were actually inclusions that impacted your shine factor. When you see a diamond, you may think it's perfect, but no diamond is perfect. When a diamond comes out of the rough, the person who found it, the creator of the diamond, may have let it sit there for a while and appreciated the beauty. Sooner or later, the person looks at that diamond and starts imagining what else the diamond can be, how else it can be shaped, and where else it can be placed. The different facets in a diamond make it shine brighter. Moreover, the different inclusions are going to be kept because if it's cut out of that diamond, the character is gone—just like you.

Take a moment to take an inventory of your life from the time you can remember. Take an inventory of the different facets in your life that changed you, that made you stop believing in yourself, that made you look at a different side of the story. Think about all of those facets year by year. Your goals, plans, accomplishments and celebrations all matter! Write them down and appreciate all that you've been through. Appreciate how far you've come. Recall what you did to breakthrough, and then find a way to imagine what else you can do. What else can you do with the power within you?

Similar to diamonds, each of us were fearfully, wonderfully, and purposefully created to live the life we want according to God's plans and purposes for us. Unfortunately, most women don't get to live a life of true fulfillment wherein love conquers all and joy, peace, and happiness is manifested through them. Instead, they live a life of scarcity, devastation, and negativity, looking for a hero to wipe all their tears away instead of tapping into the inner power that strengthens them to live better days. When you pick and choose how you show up because of people, you diminish the vision of an all-knowing God who planned and purposed you to be who you are—a light that shines on this side of heaven. Keep in mind that different parts of you can be used in different ways because the makers can also re-cut you.

The re-cutting is hard, but you have to be still in the

moment of that process to understand and appreciate what you were going through. You can't rush it. You just have to trust it. You can't push it. You just have to be still. There's no set time or set moment. You know when it's over because you can appreciate the brilliance that comes through. If you haven't yet appreciated the brilliance that comes through from your stillness, from the time you have to be re-cut for another position in your life, another level in your life, or like a diamond, another setting in your life, then be still and appreciate that there's more that God wants to do for you. He wants you to be still in this moment and appreciate that He's got it under control. He's already pre-ordained. He already knows where you're going to be. He's already expected where you're going to go. He already knows the facet and inclusion that's going to come out and make you shine brighter after the cut.

We don't always like those obstacles, but obstacles are facets of your life, as well. Usually, after we get through those obstacles and the opposition, we understand another inclusion that we didn't know. I always ran from the obstacles because when I was growing up, obstacles were demonized. Stop demonizing what you don't know and start looking at it, looking down upon it, and saying, "If there is an obstacle, then there's something that I need to appreciate about me." Sit still long enough to appreciate the following things. What is the lesson? What is the message? What is the next thing you need to understand and get from this level to get to the next level? Keep your eyes on the prize of pressing forward to get what is ahead of you. Seek to see how to make your latter greater. Seek a peak at what could be if you don't stop but instead keep pushing forward for bigger, better, and more.

What is keeping you from making your hopes and dreams come true? Perfect timing? No time is perfect, so you must start when you feel the pulling at your heart, even if you don't think you are ready. As you walk by faith to satisfy an insatiable craving for more, you will stumble upon people, places, and things that will motivate you to keep doing, keep pursuing, and keep moving towards your hopes, dreams, unlimited possibilities, and destiny. You have been designed for such a time as this. Anytime your heart moves you, that's the time to shine. Anytime your spirit moves you, that's the time to shine. Anytime your feet start walking before your mouth starts talking, that is the time to shine. You're designed to shine. So, don't dull who you are. Don't remove or cover up your shimmer. You are supposed to be the salt of the earth. You are supposed to be an instrument of success. You are supposed to be a fisher of men. So, embrace who you are. Be the person that they want to be, who they want to bless, and the person they want to admire so that you can make change possible.

You must say "yes" throughout the process of upleveling your mindset and success. Say yes to the opposition. Say yes to the tests. Say yes to negativity. Say yes to the things you think are going to defeat you. Say yes to the things you don't want to do. When you say yes, you make yourself stronger deep down on the inside. When you say yes, your experience shifts for you. When your experience shifts for you, you get stronger, and you always allow yourself to breakthrough. When you say yes to yourself, you will get to where you need to be. You will even get to where you were meant to be. When you say yes, you'll say yes to the point that you feel you are broken. But nothing can break you. You must say yes to your position, knowing that if God wants you somewhere else, He can re-cut you and put you in another place. You must say yes! You've got to say yes to that brilliance that wants to shine through because the Bible says, "Let your light shine."

When you let your light shine, you understand and appreciate that everything about you is not wasted. All the facets in you were not anyone's mistake. God can make good of it. All the inclusions, He knows what he's doing. He knows that even if you make a mistake, you are just like the prodigal child who can come back. And when you come back, He can re-cut, reshape, re-fix you, reposition, and replace what was taken away from you. God can embolden you and make His countenance shine upon you, no matter where you've ever been. His countenance can always shine upon you. You can always be who you always wanted to be because all you want to be is who you're meant to be—the spark that will set you free. I want you to understand that people can annoy you, limit you, stop you, and block you, but they can't break you. Never forget you're like a diamond; you can't be broken. You're meant to shine boldly, beautifully, and brilliantly forever.

However, in picking and choosing how you show up, you diminish the vision of an all-knowing God who planned and purposed you to be who you are. I can tell you how I suffered from eating disorders, slouched in hopes of being smaller, and hid behind personalities in hopes of trying to get in where I wasn't meant to fit in, but I won't. Instead, I will inspire a desire in you to appreciate that someone is going through what you grew through. Perhaps you went through a prodigal son/daughter experience where you demanded to live your life on your terms, but you turned your life around. Or you got a second leash on life after you attempted to commit suicide on several occasions because of a breakup. Or you found a way to increase your profits after you went to family, lawyers, preachers and whosoever because of a financial crisis or recent diagnosis.

Your story matters. You must enlighten this world with the light within you that has been shaped by your experience. Now that you know what to do, you can help others avoid going down the dead ends you learned to avoid. So, shine your light through the darkness to help others break free from the lies of life and the strongholds of sameness. Never forget, when God said let your light shine, He was speaking of you, too! You must allow yourself not only to be blessed and highly favored but also blessed and bankable. You have the power to bank your brilliance. Whether your brilliance is encapsulated into a book, a class, video series, life lessons, a song, dance, or music, you must create more than you consume. You help others as you help yourself. By standing in your power, you empower yourself to enlighten the world so that what you went through doesn't serve as a stumbling block to others. You are a walking epistle read by men, women, and children. You are the evidence that people can point to. You were hurt, healed, and made whole who now serves as the evidence that God's word is true. God provides the provision for His vision.

Once you fully appreciate that the light tucked into the belly of your soul is a piece of God, you will stop trying to dimmer it. You will appreciate the price many have paid who came before you so you can shine. You will stop devaluing yourself and start embracing the fact that you are more priceless than rubies. All of the pressure, pain, and hell you went through helps you shine the light within you. So, no matter what you have been through, shine your light! No matter the size and shape you are in, shine your light anyway. People assigned to you won't see what they need to see if you don't shine your light. They won't get a chance to bump into the evidence that they can hope for more.

Find Your Tribe

When I started my own professional career path and entrepreneurship, I didn't realize my momma's story, societal norms, and more would impact my life. I watched and waited for someone to support me, but none did. I thought I needed someone to validate me as John the Baptist validated Jesus, but none did. I thought I would overwork myself into the rooms I wanted to be in, but I ended up being treated as a doormat. I thought I could swipe my credit card to my way to success, but no matter how much I tried, I could not cheat my way to success. I kept trying to be better, speak better, show up better; I was driven not to be the foster kid of success. However, I found myself becoming the very thing I didn't want to be. I knew I wanted to be successful, but I wasn't definitive. I didn't know where I was going. I didn't know where I wanted to go. But I knew I didn't want to go back to the urban hood where I came from. So, I did what I learned to do, which was complain about what I didn't have.

A few times, I raised my hand to volunteer to help women and kids live better than I learned to live. But maybe my walk, my talk, my look, or my unwillingness to be controlled made people reject me. Or at least that was their excuse. After one too many rejections, I stopped raising my hand. Instead, I resolved to live my life, sleep through the weekends, and schedule my vacations just like everyone else. People talked about me, borrowed from me, used me, and skipped over me. And I stopped caring. My not caring changed when I almost died from a medical error wherein I had an ectopic pregnancy, and the doctors failed to give me a DNC. But for the grace of God, giving me a dream that I was pregnant with twins, I probably wouldn't be alive. After I went through three cycles of Methotrexate to clear out the dead tissue that multiplied in my body, I asked God to give me a second chance to live. I was no longer hostage to my story of being physically, sexually, and financially abused. As a result of asking God to give me a second chance at life, I eventually started over. I stopped looking for a hero, and I started becoming who I needed to be to stop living by default and start living by design.

I started setting boundaries around my brilliance. I began to decree and declare what I wanted, and I started giving myself permission to bank myself. A few years later, I emerged as the best version of myself...or so I thought. A few years after I declared my emancipation from being a doormat to my doubt, fear, and insecurities, one of my sisters passed away. Unbeknownst to me, she stopped being the independent woman I had known her to be and started becoming an abused woman. But instead of crying and leaving, she decided to fight back. She fought a good fight before she died. When baby girl passed away, a piece of me died with her. In truth, I lived on autopilot for over a year because I couldn't believe she was gone. She had empowered so many women, made money to help others bury their children, and managed to go from working minimum wage jobs to making almost thirty dollars an hour. My sister was focused and even started going back to church. But when she died, she was living beneath her God-given privileges. I was confused, disappointed, and emotionally drained.

A year after my most favorite sister passed away, God told me that I could take center stage. I had never been at the forefront of my success. I had lived in a story where I was the sidechick. I researched, developed, and whispered strategies to others; I led from the background. But after I got the Holy Instant download, I knew within the soul of my existence that it was my turn to lead. I stopped asking and started leading. I created Diva Moment, a nonprofit organization to help women activate their leadership and own their power to bank themselves. I didn't know what I was doing; I just wanted to help. Once a month, I opened up a monthly talk over breakfast to discuss how women could uplevel their success. For over eighteen months, breakfast was free. Some people showed up, some didn't, and others ignored my invitations. During my last meeting, I met a woman who I still call my friend today. If I had said yes to my failed group empowerment gathering, I wouldn't have met my friend who introduced me to a network of businesswomen who needed and appreciated my skills.

Upon meeting my entrepreneurial sisters, who were both Kingdom-minded and mission-driven, something within me upleveled. I could never go back to the bad teaching that kept me stuck. I realized that what I did to get to where I was could never help me get to where God created me to be. I knew where I wanted to be. And I knew who I needed to be. But instead of looking for a savior or excuse, I became obsessed with getting to where I wanted to be. As I started obsessing about what I wanted, I negated other people's opinions and prioritized what I felt I deserved. I submitted to the process of being a better Toni in life and in business. In doing so, my returns on investment began to increase. I'm not going to lie and say it was easy. I'm not going to pretend like my life shifted in twenty-one days. I'm not even going to persuade you that everyone loved the unbossed Toni. But I started liking me.

You were fearfully and wonderfully created to be a divinely inspired vocal agent of change who can speak what she seeks to fulfill a greater destiny. But you may not know your power. In fact, most of us have not been cultivated to shine our light, but to dimmer our shine and follow a parent, teacher, friend, pastor, influencer, and/or celebrity. We were cultivated to consume more than to create. We have been cultivated to be scriveners more than strategists, and we were cultivated to be who society wants us to be more than who God created us to be. Hence why the power to manifest heaven here on Earth lies dormant. But when you know within your soul that nothing happens until something happens, you seek wisdom.

Much like a diamond in the rough, you needed to be dug out of your rock-bottom situation. You need to be loved and appreciated for your character, class, and qualities. You needed to be molded, shaped, and polished to perfection. There are many facets throughout your life that need to be polished to perfection—different sides, different shades, and, believe it or not, character flaws. Ever since the day of your birth, you shined brightly to someone. Within each moment of your life, another facet was discovered. Even in the heat of the moment when you said something out of character, you were able to discover another side of you. No one in your family could mold and shape the shine within you but you. When your journey of self-discovery helps in knowing your sparkle, your energy, your reliance, and your tribe, you will be able to uplevel in every aspect of your life.

As a child, I decided I didn't want to be like my momma. To ensure it was so, I found another mother who served and still serves as my godmother. While she went to church, she still defined her reality and shaped her own destiny. She had a job, traveled the world, and shifted her existence from a small-town game. She changed to an amazing fashion designer and event planner. I even tried to jump from my house to her house as a child, but each time I was with her, our time together was short. Even a short impression dies hard, though. I stumbled upon my propensity to monetize by brilliance by accident. When I was ten, I discovered my ability to bankroll myself by babysitting, cleaning kitchens, and bathrooms. In my teens, I had several babysitting jobs and worked at a job so I didn't have to ask for money. In college, I worked several part-time jobs, started a few failed side hustles, seriously considered working as an escort, and interviewed as a phone sex operator, but I didn't get the job. Unfortunately, or fortunately, I never had a father who would or could give me everything I needed. Nor did I meet a sugar daddy, or mama, who was willing to take my absentee's daddy's place.

I discovered the tribe of workaholics who believed that their work would set them free from poverty. While hanging with them, I discovered that their god was a job that gave them hundreds of thousands of dollars, a personal phone, a personal line of credit, a travel card, and access to the point system through travel. Their job also gave them Golden Handcuffs, Deferred Income Privileges, and a parachute if their ties were severed. I aspired to be like them until I realized I hardly saw my husband, and they frowned at my need to attend worship service and lead a team in ministry. The longer I hung with them, the more I understood the meaning of "what profits a man to lose their soul".

For over fifteen years, I ran far away from the wisdom of the Bible while sitting, praying, and teaching in the church. I didn't like how my momma practiced Christianity, and I didn't like how it was taught. So, I went through life getting the degrees, jobs, and influence while reading around the Bible. Between *My Daily Bread*, Thursday night service, and several church services on Sunday, I was good. Or so I thought until I found myself in a place that my Ivy League education and material possessions couldn't take me, pleading the Blood of Jesus to have a second chance at living my best life. Once I was willing to step out of my comfort zone to live my best life, I found that I was living my best life here on Earth. So, I upleveled.

Faith It to Make It

Is your faith messing you up or manifesting greater things for you? We've heard all of our favorite pastors say the same thing. "Find your lane!" "There's no competition in your lane." "There's a lane that God created exclusively for you." I have said variations of these very phrases, but I know for sure you are Bossed AND Bankable because you were created by the Most-High God to live, love, and lead your best life limitlessly on this side of heaven. Don't allow your belief in God to make you feel entitled to His protection from disappointment. Faith doesn't work like that. Whether in life or business, rock bottom will lead you to where your parents, teachers, pastors, evangelists, and mentors can't—a spirit-to-spirit encounter with God.

I'm a self-help girl. I've been helping myself for as long as

I can remember. As a child, I tried to convince my mama that she could overcome financial slavery that kept her shackled to menial jobs, in shelters, begging for breadcrumbs, and living beneath her God-given privileges. But despite Momma lying prostrate, praying to God, attending church conferences, and showing up to church as much as seven days a week, she died impoverished. My momma had the skills to pay her bills, but she never tapped into her ability to economize or even multiply her finances. To avoid living as my momma, I became a "two tears in a bucket" kind of chick. I rolled with the dealers, complained about men only wanting my sweet and gushy, and always told people I was looking for a sugar daddy while trying to stretch ten dollars for a week. I hated my life. I was failing myself and always found myself repeating the same narrative on a different day. Even when I upleveled from college student to grad student, I was on the vicious wheel of trying, failing, and starting over. Even when I started my legal career, my life was miserable because I was living better than I ever had, but it didn't reflect my dreams.

Through trials, tribulations, and life experiences, I learned to scratch, survive, and be grateful for what comes my way because I was unworthy. I was unworthy of grace, favor, love, blessings, and God's overflow because of who I came from, who I was, and what I did. I had fallen so far from being who I thought I could be that I started pulling away from the very people who expected more from me. I stopped hoping and dreaming. I stopped doing whatever I could to escape from my reality. I just stopped trying to be someone I wanted to become and just succumbed to my reality.

Bad spiritual teaching fueled with judgment will cause you

to live within the status quo so much that you fail to become the fullest version of yourself. You fail to advocate for yourself. You allow low vibration people to have more to say about your destiny than you, and you wind up living beneath your Godly potential rather than redefining it. I've been there, done that, sabotaged myself, silenced myself, shrouded myself, circled the drain of despair, dimmed my shine, and have T-shirts that testify of my redundancy. But what I learned during my path of crawling from the basement to other people's boardrooms is that no weapon formed against us shall prosper. Other people's words, threats, judgment, abuse, rejection, nor Facebook blocking can hurt you. In fact, it's merely a facade; false evidence appearing real to keep you stuck in fear instead of slaying by faith.

Prior to reading pieces of *A Course in Miracles*, I had sent myself to hell and back several times because of bad teaching. Just a few chapters in, and I realized I had been taught wrong by loving people who didn't know better. As I began reading the book, I realized God wasn't a bully. God was a loving father who had empowered me to wake up to my potential, wake up to where I was meant to be, and to wake up to the fact that I needed help. I was triggered by the fact that God was love and that I needed to look at my relationship with Him through the lens of love. God wasn't counting my sins to rebuke and chastise me. Instead, he was a Father who loved me, opened and closed doors for me, and directed and redirected me. Similarly, pastors, clergy, teachers, preachers, influencers, millionaires, and billionaires weren't better than me. Instead, they were brothers and sisters who were on a mission to have, do, and be more on this side of heaven.

I began to appreciate that miracles were a changed mind, which was totally different than the doctrine I heard and was never taught. Needless to say, the book, *A Course in Miracles*, changed my life. Prior to reading parts of the book, I had demonized myself so much that I couldn't fully appreciate my potential. As a child, I was taught that bad girls went to hell. So, as a grown woman, parts of me thought that I was too good to fail but not worthy of soaring. As I walked *through A Course in Miracles*, I began studying the Law of Attraction, which led me to read my Bible differently. I no longer wanted my faith to be molded and shaped by people who didn't fully appreciate that God gave us the power to work out our own salvation with fear and trembling. So, I started questioning my intention and started disconnecting from individuals who weren't chasing a dream that defied their reality.

In Matthew 9:29, God healed that man according to his faith. Whether good, bad, or indifferent, our faith manifests much. You shall receive according to your faith in surviving, maintaining, or living day by day. Let it be to you. In the alternative, according to your faith of being blessed, bankable, favored, anointed, healed, whole, and worthy, let it be to you. Once, I realized we get to choose whether to live according to what we were taught or according to what we believe in our heart, those things God has for us. Whether we are inspired to forgive or forbade, to receive or repel, we get to choose how to live our best life. You must force yourself to uplevel your faith to overcome misunderstandings, miseducation, missiles of spiritual war, and mistakes. In order to manifest success in every aspect of your life, you can't be so in love with what you have been through, gone through, identified with, or what you've learned to be content with. You are never too old to manifest success for yourself. Nor should you ever be so busy that you don't have the time to bless yourself. We're told to make faith bigger, but what is faith to someone who's tried, stumbled, fell, and persuaded by others not to get back up?

The trick to achieving greater success is breaking through mental blocks, breaking through strongholds, and name and claim dreams within each moment of our everyday lives. The more you seek better, pursue greater things, and do more, the more you begin to believe in yourself again. The more you believe, the more you achieve, which inspires you to take steps towards greatness. The further you distance yourself from the fear of not having and not doing, the more powerful you become. Once you get to the edge of your reality, your zip codes, families, and egoic tendencies, the more you begin to believe you can do anything. God has given you the authority to manifest better, greater, and more from you through you. You should already know the path to success will not be easy. If it were so easy, most of us wouldn't stop, stumble, fall, and regress to what we know and possibly try again throughout our lives.

To manifest into the fullness of who God says you are, you will have to lose some friends. Everyone is not meant to go where God has preordained for you to go. You may lose money as you seek, know, ask, and try to follow the wrong path and wrong people. You may even feel like you're losing your mind. I know I did because I kept knocking at the door and showing up to the same resource until I learned the lesson that I had missed in my naiveté, which was that I was responsible for following God's tugs, pulls, and whispers.

Thankfully, when your mind, body, and spirit are in sync with God's purpose and plans for your life, you feel as though you really have a reason for living. Your voice is clear, your judgment is sound, your passion is contagious, and you are inspired to live more, love more, and do more. And when you choose to share, it's no longer burdensome but actually a natural response to God's goodness, mercy, and grace.

Once you are committed to becoming who God created you to be, another's judgment won't matter, another's deception won't matter, another's rejection won't matter, another's deceit won't matter, and another's harsh words won't matter. The only thing that matters is protecting your spirit from the things of the world in order to become the miracle you were meant to be. In effect, you become open to the possibility that your eyes may not have seen it all, and your ears may not have heard all of the good things God has in store for you. You allow yourself to become more open to any shifts in the atmosphere and less tolerant of the same ole same or the status quo. Even when others are willing to wait, be still, be complacent in their circumstance, you must press forward to the rhythmic cadence of your beating heart.

In seeking, knowing, and appreciating your power to manifest greater things, you must stop allowing pains to have power over you. You must also stop allowing your emotions to eviscerate what God spoke over you. Instead, you must start recognizing the signs, wonders, and miracles of pursuing things outside of your comfort zone. You must start seeking opportunities that your focus on not having would have been kept from you. In effect, you tap into a more evolved, spiritual, and wiser part of yourself that knows God's truth and Word.

You will press towards the prize of your high calling of living, loving, and leading your legacy as the queen that you are.

The miracle within you needs for you to seek, know, nurture, and cultivate it through words, actions, and belief. Your miracle place is higher than you've ever been before with that place in that space that allows you to have governance. Your presence is the governance that allows you to give you this day, the daily bread, so that you're not scratching and surviving. You're not posting and praying, but you're positioning yourself to be a better version of yourself. The added bonus is that you will fully appreciate the people, places, and things that will help you uplevel out of a fixed mentality. You'll become more than the status quo! You'll be the one who can make your dreams possible! You'll position yourself to be the provision. You'll position yourself to be the miracle worker. You'll position yourself to become the trailblazer of your success.

Lastly, in this higher level of being, you will find yourself seeking more of God's wisdom to help you achieve more. As God continuously helps you achieve more, you start believing in yourself. In so doing, you start to appreciate the possibility within you. The more you believe in yourself and appreciate yourself, you unlock and unleash your personal power, which empowers you to be more than anything you have endured or encountered to ensure your hopes and dreams become a reality. Believe me when I say if it doesn't feel right in your spirit, it is not meant for you. Instead of adhering to what other people have said, unchain yourself from societal norms and mores. Declare your freedom over the principalities that make you tiptoe in faith and show up as a mere shadow of your possibilities. Tap into the Holy Ghost's amazing power that lets you appreciate that you can do all things. You can overcome obstacles, spread your winds of creativity, and defy the strongholds that have crushed a greater legacy in your generation.

Use your mouth to speak what you seek. Write your vision of having, doing, and being more than you've ever seen before. Do whatever it takes to command your faith to manifest greater in every aspect of your life. I'm a living testimony to the fact that those holy instances will cause you to shift how you see and experience life circumstances. Similarly, the Holy Spirit will lead, guide, direct, and pull you to do what's needed to get into position for God's provisions. However, if you aren't taught to be a leader but a follower, your holy sense will be dulled. Similarly, if you're not taught how to be fruitful and multiply, you will never activate your inner glow to make your dreams possible. You don't need anyone's permission to bless you. In fact, God has given you the power to become who you need to be to live a greater legacy. Do you believe you are blessed with the tools to pick up your own mat, mind, ability, and talent? When you look back over your life, can you fully appreciate when the Holy Spirit gave you an opportunity to shift your footstep?

You have been masterfully created in the likeness of an infinite, all-powerful, all-encompassing, and all-knowing God who breathed a divine assignment into your spirit before you were a twinkle in anyone's eyes. In order to help you go where you have never been before, see what you have never seen before, and do what you have never done before, you must tap into the fullness of who you are. However, your gifts and talents are not enough to help you be more without God. Life gets in the way, circumstances get in the way, situations get in the way, and people get in the way. Just know, if you can dream it, you can be it. You can overcome more if you don't forget that the problems, excuses, pain, and negativity are merely obstacles blocking your vision.

Don't diminish your ability to overcome. As you overcome more, you empower yourself to do more. In effect, you begin to do more of what you have never done before, which motivates you to work in purpose towards a dream that you had never dreamed of before. By walking by faith towards your dream, you find yourself seeking more of God's wisdom to help you achieve more. As God continuously helps you achieve more, you start believing in yourself, which ultimately helps you appreciate that you are meant for more. The more you believe in yourself and appreciate yourself, you unlock and unleash your personal power, which empowers you to be more than anything you have endured or encountered to ensure your hopes and dreams become a reality. Take the first step by defining what makes life meaningful to you, your children, and your children's children.

Show Up for Success

There comes a time in our lives that we find ourselves wondering how we got here, why we continually do what we do, or how we can start over. I know what it's like to live in fear of getting into yet another bad situation. Whether getting a butt whooping, getting ejected from a circle of influencers, or getting a phone call that ruins everything. I found myself in a constant, never-ending cycle of doing and being in fear of getting ejected. If you're over thirteen years old, I'm sure you've already experienced times of failure, fear, and fabulosity. In each situation, your experience didn't last. Sometimes your experience felt fleeting, but it didn't stop you from seeking, knowing, and asking for more. In fact, nothing can stop you from becoming who you're meant to be. Like a seed growing next to water, your spirit will find a way to quench its thirst. Much like an acorn that grows on oak trees, your possibilities are limitless. You're a catalyst for change, a trailblazer that blazes new trails, and you have the power within you to make change possible. You must seek, know, and ask what's next.

Unfortunately, if you continually ignore what makes you cry and keep you up at night, you limit yourself from being healed from deep down on the inside. Whether you experienced sexual abuse, physical abuse, trauma, or mental abandonment, you must deal with the problem so you can heal from the wound and uplevel to new levels throughout your life. In order to heal from the pain, you must commit to the process of healing, which is much like surgery, wherein you must seek, discover, and assess the root of your pain. In so doing, you become more like a researcher who seeks to know why you live your life as though you don't matter, why you're seemingly unworthy of manifesting your dreams, and why you continually allow your mind, body, and spirit to be used as a receptacle for others to insert, push, and release their negativity, bitterness, and emptiness into you before you can even think of reaching the peak of your own fulfillment.

Each of us has the power to define who we are despite the names we are called, despite the life situations we face, or despite how others try to mold us into who they think we should be. In life, we need to be two things: who we are and who we want to be. The thoughts we think become the things we believe, which affects the choices we make. For some, obstacles look like opportunities, whereas in other instances, opportunities feel more like obstacles. Similarly, blessings feel more like an unshakeable curse, whereas some things we thought would work out for our good ended up become the very things that forced us to give in most of the time. When I talk to people about their frustrations, they focus on the other person. But I always ask them, "What do you see? Take your emotions out of that story. What do you see?" And now I ask you, what keeps showing up all the time? Because whatever keeps showing up is the lesson you need to learn.

In the Bible, we know about the story of Moses and the burning bush. The crazy thing is I didn't know this until I heard T.D. Jakes say it in one of his sermons that Moses lived in a desert, and bushes burned all the time. But it was something about the bush that made Moses stop. See, most of us see something all the time, and we don't appreciate that there could be a message. Stop yourself long enough so you can appreciate that something is missing. Seek, know, and ask what you have missed before that you now need to focus on. If you don't know, ask God. Literally, open your mouth and ask God for grace, guidance, and action steps. Whenever you get stopped, seek God's guidance so that you live, have, breathe, and do His perfect will more than His permissive one. You have been given a divine assignment to make our world better. However, whether or not we fulfill our mission is based on whether we are guided by our inner victim or inner victor throughout our life journey.

Our inner victim aka ego, deafens our ears, which prevents us hearing Spirit's leadings, guidance, and comfort. Being led by your inner victim will ensure that don't know who you are, love who you are, or appreciate who you are. You will find yourself struggling with accepting that you can live the life you choose to live. If you are continually looking outside of yourself for permission to do what God has commissioned, or if you are struggling with the idea that you are more than enough to manifest your hopes and dreams, then it is time to empower your expectations. Oftentimes, we stunt our ability to live the life we love based upon facts, figures, and statistical reports. In effect, we live one day at a time scratching, surviving, and just holding on in hopes of being rescued by another someday just as generations before us had done.

Seemingly, those who find themselves in their endless cycle of watching and waiting are not completely at fault since we aren't taught how to proactively live our best life. We are persuaded, cultivated, and encouraged to merely survive it. But, thankfully, God finds a way to motivate each of us to seek better to change our stories despite our starting points. No one on this earth can help you be who God created you to be other than you. From the beginning to the end, you have been given trials, tribulations, and lessons that were not meant to break you but help you appreciate what God put in you. Each day offers new blessings, mercies, and opportunities to give you hope that something more is in store. Regardless of what your eyes see, follow your heart, which serves as a divine beacon that leads you, guides you, and encourages you to seek better, demand greater, and pursue more. Whether parent, child, family, teacher, preacher, lover, or boss, hurt people leave a trail of tears and scarred souls.

You don't have to stay stuck in your unhealed spiritual wounds. When I learned that we always get what we focuse on, I stopped fixating on what happened, who wouldn't let me, or who didn't want me. Instead, I started focusing on my heart, my mind, my dreams, and my goals. I began asking God to give me daily bread to live my best life, and I became fixated on becoming the woman of my dreams. Similarly, you must allow more to come through you. Whether through your life, your family, your job, or business, more must come through you. Even when fear shows up, more must come through you. Or if you're lying in your bed wondering why you fell for the lies throughout your life more than God's promises of purpose, power, provisions, purpose, and prosperity. Your ability to affect your own life and the world around you is limitless. Whether that effect is positive or negative depends on you. Believing in yourself is the foundation of your success. This comes from knowing who you are. You must be conscious of the fact that you are best served by appreciating God's truth— learning to recognize the truth or absence of it in yourself and others. You are at the center of your story. Your world will thrive and so will those with whom you connect regardless of how you are connected. Your ability to balance energy is essential to empowered living. So, you must learn when to ask for help and when to have the courage to try on your own. Both are important.

Attaining success in all areas of life stems from discovering your true identity. Your ability to show up in this world is limitless. You have the potential, passion, purpose, and power to make change possible for you. In fact, God has preordained you to let your light shine, to live your best life, to be fruitful and multiple, and to dominate in every aspect of your life. You get to choose your existence here on Earth. You can turn a pitiful story into a powerful one. You can turn your anger into activated activity. You can change your world by changing your words. When you spend time on focusing on what you see more than what could be, you miss out on the opportunity to be more. However, when you know who you are, no good thing can be denied from you—peace, love, happiness, and worthiness.

You must negate the negativity that pacifies your soul to be still, to be content, to wait for the perfect time, and/or to wait on God to do what He expects you to do. Instead, you must forge your destiny to be who God created you to be. Similarly, when you're in situations in life wherein you are dimming your shine to survive, you must assess yourself. You must determine if what you're doing will keep you broke, busted, and disgusted, or if it will empower you to uplevel into a better version of yourself. You're not meant to fit into spaces and places where you don't belong. Nor are you just meant to survive life. In fact, you're meant to thrive in your life so you can grow into the fullest version of yourself.

Never forget, thoughts are things that either make you or break you. In fact, eighty percent of your success is based on the things you do six inches between your ears. So, if you don't like where you are, uplevel your mindset. Think better thoughts so you manifest greater things. Allow yourself to believe you're a seed that is meant to bloom, blossom, and grow where you're planted. Force yourself to uplevel your mindset so you don't get stuck in stories and roles God didn't give you the grace to overcome. Always give yourself permission to uplevel into your fullest potential no matter what comes your way. You don't always have to survive. You don't even have to get by. You don't even have to deny yourself, but you need to look around and see what the successful people do. When you realize what the successful people do, you realize that there is a time and a place for everything, and then everything has a time and a place. You'll also realize that there is a promise for you to be powerful, profitable, and prosperous, but you must submit to the process of becoming who God created you to be.

Never Lose Hope

I have been guilty of dreaming dreams without being accountable for them. Some are also guilty of forgiving others but do not forgive themselves. Others are guilty of attending church services and empowerment sessions without applying lessons learned. And still, others are guilty of saying we are faithful without doing the things we feel inspired to do or becoming the full manifestation of our dreams. One thing I know for sure is that God's blessings come by us, to us, and through us to help us become the person we need to be to fulfill a greater destiny. But when we fail to appreciate that we were meant to be more, seek more, and do more, we imprison our mind, body, and spirit to fear, doubt, and negativity. We also fail to unleash our possibilities to become who God created us to be. To bridge the gap between your destiny and reality, you must believe you are worthy of more. You must own the power that helps you walk right, talk right, and want to live beyond what's in sight. Also, you must commit to seeking and seizing more than ever before. Come what may, say yes to more. I always wanted to know whether I could have been who I am without going through my traumatic childhood, stumbling through the valleys of the ghetto, and being stuck at the bottom of the mountain. While God never really gave me a direct answer to my musings, He allowed me to sit back and appreciate His process that has been continual and consistent from the beginning of time. What has been pronounced from the start is that we each have a divine assignment to live more, love more, and share more pieces of heaven here on Earth. Unfortunately, we stop ourselves from being a better version of ourselves based on the negativity, obstacles, opposition, and fear we encounter—the very things that are meant to draw out what God put in.

Life is a journey wherein you must seek, find, unlock, and unleash the divine brilliance expressed into you when God created you. While we only do what we know, we get tripped up, bound up, knocked up, and locked up before we learn to appreciate that we must give up what we know and seek to become despite our realities. Don't you want more peace, joy, and happiness? Don't you want to live a life that is meaningful to you? Don't you want to make your hopes and dreams come true? If you answered yes to any of these questions, then it's time to take an inner journey to unleash the greatness within you. Throughout life, our struggles help us endure, and obstacles help us spread our creative wings to soar for more. But for the pains in our past, we would not have found our passion for what we love most or hate most that motivate our actions and activities. But for the opposition, denials, and resistance from the very people who we thought had our backs, we would not have discovered our ability to restore and motivate ourselves to seek better alternatives to become better outcomes. During those moments of seeking better, do we fully appreciate that they are meant to be greater than what our eyes have ever seen? At some point, you must free yourself from whatever belief or stronghold is holding you back to unleash the greatness within you. If you cannot unleash yourself from a life that doesn't reflect pieces of heaven on Earth, then truth will make you free.

The truth will free you from the misperceptions that kept you from moving forward. You will be free from the miseducation that kept you from elevating above and beyond your life experiences and circumstances that were meant to teach you, not mold you. You will be free from your inner me shaped by more than seven generations before you learned to live but not to be. Being free from things you know so you can soar to higher heights and deeper depths throughout life will hurt and cause you so much pain that you may question why you went through the process in the first place. But, ultimately, the truth will make you unleash and untether yourself from the spiritual wounds that served as thorns and caused you more pain. The process of discovering the source of your pain consists of taking inventory of the first time your heart bled so much that you no longer mattered to yourself.

When you walk through the wound of your soul, you must go back to the places and spaces where you stopped becoming and started doing to live. Go back to where someone muted your voice. Go back to where someone caused you to fear for your life. Go back to where you were no longer pretty to yourself. Even if you skipped through the childhood period of seek and find, adolescence period of rejection, or young adulthood of self-discovery unscathed, there will be a period wherein you started living in your broken place more than emerging as the fullness of who you are. Go back in your mind when you stopped loving yourself and started diminishing your needs and goals. Find the place where you made other people's opinions bigger than God's whispers. Just know, if you aren't currently living in your triumphs, then you are living in another's downfall—including your own. Find the place that broke you so you can break through and heal yourself from the inside out.

Your true essence is within you and praying you get to a point in your life that you grow weary with doing and instead start seeking knowledge and wisdom to become a better version of yourself. I hope you will find a way to bridge the gap between who you are and who you were born to be. To accomplish this goal, hope may present déjà vu experiences to encourage you to stay on your chosen path despite your circumstances. At other times, when life becomes unbearable, hope will allow you to stumble upon a sore spot in your life so you are given opportunities to experience God's grace that helps heal and restore you. What I know for sure, hope will never fail you, nor will it ever give up on you. Hope will continuously present opportunity after opportunity to help you appreciate your innate ability to mold and shape a more significant legacy from your thoughts, words, and actions. But when nothing else seems to help, hope will lovingly step aside to allow chaos to wreak havoc over your life in an effort for you to unlock the power within you to unleash the essence of you. Don't make life harder by living without hoping, because faith is birthed through hope. In fact, faith is the evidence of things hoped for despite not seeing, knowing, or experiencing it in your reality.

Don't focus on the fear of not being good enough, not being smart enough, not being rich enough, not being talented enough, not being popular enough, not being loved enough, and not being appreciated enough. I encourage you to look at the other side of fear. That side of fear is not living the life that you're supposed to live because your soul knows there is something more about what you're supposed to do than going day in and day out of being—the day in and day out of going to work, going to school, paying bills, finding a house, getting in more debt, finding love, and having children. There's something deep down on the inside of you that knows you were meant to do so much more than what you're doing. Even as you grew in age and experience, you were still tethered to something that kept you hoping, dreaming, and praying for something within your reach.

You are a living example of your personal testimony of how you changed your fate by changing your beliefs. No one on this earth can help you be who God created you to be other than you. From the beginning to the end, you have been given trials, tribulations, and lessons that were not meant to break you but to help you appreciate what God put in you. Similarly, each day offered new blessings, mercies, and opportunities to give you hope that something more is in store. Regardless of what your eyes see, follow your heart, which serves as a divine beacon that leads you, guides you, and encourages you to seek better, demand greater, and pursue more. You're going to question why you got started in the first place. But when you work out your own financial salvation, something will shift. When you walk in your authority to be who God created you to be, you stop seeking validation. When you unleash the great woman within yourself, you uplevel to your next level. If you can dream it, you can be it. If you empower yourself to believe in the possibility of more, you become mindful that the problems, excuses, pain, and negativity are merely obstacles blocking your vision. And as you overcome more obstacles, you appreciate your ability to do more. In effect, you begin to do more of what you have never done before, which motivates you to work in purpose towards a dream that you had never dreamed of before.

Do this for you. Assess and appreciate the tugs in your heart. Be still and know what God wants you to do next. Despite the ups and downs, the ins and outs throughout life, allow yourself to go with the flow of life to follow your heart. As I eventually learned and now tell my clients and mentees, you can only change what God allows. Once you learn to accept what God allows, then you discover you are more than enough to become a more blissful version of yourself who accepts everyone as they are and appreciates everyone's God-given right to live the life they choose to lead. Once you realize you were created on purpose for a divine purpose, you allow yourself to seek more. There is no specific time in our lives when your purpose manifests, but it often ensues upon a traumatic event. In many instances, the pain we suffered in our pasts manifests as purpose. Don't wait for devastating pain or brokenness to force you to rebirth yourself into a better version of yourself. Instead, decree that today is the day you reclaim your life, story, dreams, purpose, and identity.

Fulfill Your Destiny

I grew up in church wherein I heard Bible stories of miracles, signs, and wonders that allowed others to manifest greater from their small beginnings. I waited for the perfect time to fully appreciate my specialness. When that didn't happen, I thought one of my "neighbors" would discover me and help me to appreciate my gifts, talents, purpose, and abilities. When that didn't happen, I waited for my Prince Charming to take me far, far away from my realities. While missing chance after chance to change my destiny, I found myself on the other side of dark alleys, crossing my fingers in doctors' offices, and praying others wouldn't recognize me when I was frolicking in places I knew I wasn't supposed to be. I had fallen so far from being who I thought I could be that I started pulling away from the very people who expected more from me. Even when my money, clothes, positions, social circles, influence, and life experiences changed, I found myself on the vicious wheel of life wherein I was trying, failing, and starting over. Even when I started my legal career, my life was miserable. Through trials, tribulations, miseducation, misdirection, and missteps, I had learned how to look good, but my life wasn't good. Life was so hard that I stopped expecting to thrive in it but just to get by on the other side of my disappointments.

Even some church elders and leaders made me think I was unworthy of God's grace. From the clothes I wore, the words I thought, my complaints and foul mood, I was unworthy of God's grace, mercy, and presence. I mean, even praise and worship singers sang about their unworthiness. So, I thought if the leaders who usher in the Spirit find themselves unworthy, then far be it for me to expect anything. I can attest that change is not easy. However, to achieve what you've never seen or heard before, you must respond differently to life issues and strife lessons. I stopped because every time I tried to pursue more, I faced opposition or heard, "why you doing this" and "why you doing that" or "you just don't know what you want to do" or "you ain't never satisfied."

While waiting to be discovered by the Gate Keepers of Success, I stopped being and started doing what was expected of me. Monday through Saturday, I showed up for work, clients, professors (always a student), husband, and family. Sundays after church, I rested and napped to be ready for the following workweek. A few times, I tried to uplevel my social circle by getting in and fitting in with popular people, but it never worked out. I wasn't invited to the birthday parties; I wasn't invited to the social gatherings; I wasn't invited to the barbecues, nor would they invite me to the trips out of town to see the popular televangelists. I went to seminary school, but after two and a half semesters, I knew it would be some time before I showcased that I could speak in known tongues. After I gracefully bowed out of seminary school, I began papering myself with degrees and certification. I figured if people didn't appreciate my substance, they would respect my credentials. But although I had amassed degrees and certifications, nothing superficial could appease an insatiable soul that can only be appeased by God's spirit and truth. It took me a while to understand that God had plans and purposes for me to live, love, and prosper in every aspect of my life. I'm sure it's been a while for you, too.

Life has shown me repeatedly that we hold the keys to whether we will sabotage ourselves or successfully uplevel to the spaces and places where we belong. What I know for sure, we are good. We're awesome. We're amazing. We're fearfully and wonderfully made. We have dreams. We have goals. We have the power to attain wealth. We have the power to mess over or makeover ourselves. In fact, we are more than overcomers, which means we have the power to get up more than we fall. We get to choose whether we will manifest our misery or mastery. I'm sure you've already experienced times of failure, fear, and fabulosity. In each situation, your experience didn't last. Sometimes your experience felt fleeting, but it didn't stop you from seeking, knowing, and asking for more. In fact, nothing can stop you from manifesting every good thing God spoke into your destiny but you.

Much like a tree growing next to the water, your spirit will find a way to quench its thirst. Similar to acorns that grow into oak trees, your possibilities are limitless. You're a manifestor, a force majeure, a catalyst for change, and a trailblazer that blazes new trails. You have the power within you to make change possible, and while greatness is within you, you can't manifest the greatest version of yourself by yourself. You need something higher than you to help you overcome the obstacles, opposition, and oppression within you that keeps you tethered to a status quo that serves as a millstone around your neck. God doesn't want his work to come back void. So, He will push, pull, tug, chasten, and redirect you until you stop tiptoeing in fear and start manifesting bigger, better, and more by faith.

While success leaves clues, you must walk your own pathway to success. You must learn to discern who is working for you and who's working against you. You have to identify what works for you so you can take ownership of what is birthed from your sweat equity and million-dollar mindset. What is your sweet spot, and what is not so good? What do you have the grace to do, and what don't you have the grace to do? While God's grace is sufficient, you must fully seek, know, and understand what triggers you to ensure you don't unconsciously sabotage your success. You need to change your story by changing your narrative of seeking, hoping, praying, and waiting for the perfect person, place, time, or event for you to become amazing. Believe me when I say God will never allow anyone to do for you what you are meant to do for yourself.

Much like a baby who has to learn how to walk on its own or a toddler who has to learn how to feed herself, you must discover the power of self-efficiency. It's a process. It's not something that happens immediately. It's not something where God just wakes you up one day, and all of a sudden, it works out for your good. At the end of the day, you'll need to go through a spiritual makeover that includes trials, tribulations, and hard situations so you can fully manifest the brilliance that lies deep within you. In so doing, you must go deep within your soul to determine what keeps you stuck and what helps you soar. You need to go deep within to the place where you stopped hoping, dreaming, positioning, and expecting more to happen. Much like I had to do, you need to go to the hidden place where you got stuck and speak life to it. Go to the very place wherein you stopped advocating for better, greater, and more, and start decreeing and declaring what shall come from you. You must literally go to the root of your spiritual wounds and speak healing over it. In allowing a person or event to stop you, you disconnected yourself from your power to manifest greater. In effect, the helping place became the hurt place that served as a haunted place that buried your hopes, dreams, and possibilities.

If you don't learn for yourself or glean from others how to heal yourself, you will eventually stumble on a path where no one can awaken the potential within you—including you. You must present your full self to your life experience. Even if you don't have supporters, cheerleaders, or a yellow brick road of success, you must allow yourself to grow into your fullest potential. Much like a butterfly that is spreading its wings for the first time, you must break yourself out of the cocoon that holds you back. Within each moment of every day, spread your creative wings to soar. Through the storms of life and rain of despair, spread your wings to go higher. Don't wallow in the dark; force yourself to fly toward the silver lining. When all else fails, be like a butterfly that must leave the past behind by spreading her wings to soar for more than she's ever seen or heard before.

Think Like a Millionairess

Thinking like a millionairess is oftentimes hard to do especially if you were reared in poverty. My momma was talented, but she didn't know how to bankroll her brilliance so she could manifest her money miracles. Despite Momma's brilliance in cooking, cleaning, sewing, and creating, she spent most of her adulthood living below the poverty line. Similarly, one of my sisters didn't know how bankable she was. So, she died trying to get the attention of an older gentlemen who was her father figure, financier, and a lover. Another sister didn't know how bankable she was. So, when she found herself serving as her husband's punching bag, she felt compelled to stay until she died. Although I had degrees and specialized training, I unfortunately didn't escape the curse of living just over broke.

No one taught me to fully bankroll my brilliance in business. In effect, I bartered my worth, worked for pennies on the dollar, and never made enough to have more money than month. I mean, money was demonized, skills were abused, and gifts were never cultivated to be monetized. So, I continually did what I was cultivated to do. I bartered my brilliance, undervalued my worth, and failed to raise my financial vibration so much so that I sabotaged myself and was forced to abort business dream after business dream. That is until I complained to the Lord, and He reminded me that I had to tap into my power to attain wealth. At first, I tried to suppress the hunger and thirst for more with something I knew, but what I knew wasn't good enough. Then I tried to reach out to family and friends to understand what was happening to me. Eventually, their chatter wasn't sufficient because even though they had tons of information, what they offered wasn't filling.

You might get into a space or place wherein what you know is no longer good. You might find yourself with quadruple income in one season. You might stumble upon a vendor, a service provider, or something that makes the struggle of growing and enterprising yourself seem as easy as taking candy from a baby or selling water to thirsty members of an outdoor gym. But you have a God-given talent to increase wealth. In thinking like a millionairess, your financial goal should be more than getting out of debt and saving your latte, vacation, and hairdresser money for retirement. The ultimate concept of manifesting your money miracles is about testing and trusting God so you use your gifts and talents to transform your financial legacy into legacy wealth through the accumulation of assets, property, investments, partnership, and equity.

In addition to reducing your debt, increasing your assets, and being strategic about leveraging your assets, you must fully appreciate that you have what it takes to manifest the promises of God. Once you assess your current relationship with money and write down your vision of your dream relationship with it, then you are a lot closer to upleveling your money game. Unfortunately, most people's relationship with money stems from what they learned about money as a child. However, to uplevel your money game, you must develop a committed relationship with becoming more knowledgeable about building and protecting legacy wealth. You must learn what others have been taught. You must breakthrough the limited knowledge of financial literacy and become committed to transforming the trajectory of your financial legacy by adding, subtracting, dividing, and multiplying your gifts, talents, and knowledge.

In thinking like a millionairess, you must allow yourself to believe you are the head and not the tail in every aspect of your life. You must position yourself to be the leader and not one who is always being led to the cash register, car dealership, or anywhere else you may be triggered to spend your money. You must think of money as a blessing in that it answers all things and, much like wisdom, is duty-bound to protect you. Because money is meant to protect, support, and empower you to prosper, the devil will continually send his assailants to trigger you to spend and expend all until there is nothing left with you. You must also stop using money to define yourself. I completely understand if you don't want to agree with me on this line of thinking because seemingly everyone you know, like, and trust flaunts their money by showcasing the things they bought. I mean, the entertainers, athletes, actors, and dare I say preachers, boast about what they have, where they went, and where they will go. None of that should matter to you if you are committed to increasing your net worth and manifesting money miracles that allow you to create the type of money that blesses more than burdens you.

You get to choose whether money will serve as a weapon used against you. Alternatively, you can decide whether money is your servant that shields you, feeds you, opens doors, loosens shackles, and allows more dreams to become realities. You must also be a God pleaser more than a people pleaser. God is not pleased with you expending money to get those you idolize and worship to know, like, and trust you. In thinking like a millionairess, you focus more on the bottom line than red bottom. You seek to create more than you consume, and you find ways to leverage your income so your money blooms, blossoms, and grows for you. Third, you must position yourself to live above your circumstances and not beneath your Godly privileges. Accordingly, you must take steps to decrease your debt so you don't get stuck in the financial status quo of debt, poverty, Medicaid, bankruptcy, and governmental stipends.

Similarly, you must allow your business to be a blessing more than a curse so you live in abundance and overflow that allows you to serve as a philanthropist. When growing a business that blesses you, you tap into the brilliance within you that helps you create a product or service one time and monetize for a lifetime. Whether that is a business service or product, I want you to think in units, uniqueness, and assignment.

Don't get stuck on who doesn't like you or won't support you. Instead, focus on who can be blessed by you. Put a price on your work and continually present your offerings as a solution that helps others turn their dreams into possibilities. Once you tap into your power to manifest money miracles, you will empower yourself to be the head and not the tail, and the lender more than the borrower. As you continually think like a millionairess, you will stop looking for blessings and start being one. You will stop seeking permission to collect a commission and just expect your works to praise you. Never forget, old ways have never opened new doors. Each day, ask God to help you see what you are meant to see so you can think like a millionairess. Ask God to order your steps so you can manifest better and greater so you can achieve your million-dollar dreams that will bless you, your children and their children. Ask God to allow you to overcome the financial obstacles to make your dreams of financial freedom possible. Most importantly, ask God to keep you, bless you, and help you become unstoppable in seeking better, pursuing greater, and doing more with your money, power, and success. As you become more productive about changing your financial reality, you will empower yourself to seek better, become greater, and manifest your million-dollar dreams, brands, and businesses.

Manifest Your Success

Each of us has our own version of happily ever after etched onto our soul. During my Wealthier Empowerment Talks, I often ask women and girls what makes them special. Sadly, most responses are stutters, stammers, and long pauses instead of bold statements of faith about their specialties and/or specialness. Everyone has a specialness about them that someone is attracted to. But if you're not special to yourself, your specialness will not come shining through. Even if you are not perfect, appreciate that you are special and have the potential to become more special each day when you love yourself, forgive yourself, and believe in yourself. If nothing more, you must be bold and courageous throughout your process to become who you were meant to be.

What can you do to make your presence known? What is

the one thing you do so well that you can repetitively do and that can help us rise collectively? Do it! What can you teach so others don't sabotage their destiny? Teach that! What songs, music, and/or melody line can you hear that no one else can hear? Manifest it on this side of heaven. God has predestined and preordained you to make this world a better place. God has given you the love, power, and a strong mind to help you uplevel and emerge as the best version. Where does your help come from? Who gets you? Who's assigned to you? What tribe is aligned to your vibe? You're going to need to know if you were in this world for a reason. Seek the reason, be the reason, be the solution, and be the answer. But don't get stuck and stay where you are. Don't just watch it. Work it! Don't just hope and pray that someone will help you prevail. Stop looking for a savior. You need to take up your own mat. Understand that your mindset matters. Your abilities matter. Your talent matters. You need to pick yourself up, turn yourself around, and place your feet on solid ground so you don't get stuck in the realities of what happened. And you must continually focus on what's next.

Where do you see yourself eighteen months from now? Your brain needs a target. Many of us have a survivor mentality. We multitask, try to appease, please, and get burned out so much that we check out by vegging out. And when days become weeks, months, and eventually years, we look up and realize we are mere shadows of who we had hoped to be. We become frustrated about not getting as far as we could have, worry about whether or not we are now too old, and ultimately become spectators who continually watch, wait, and wish. But no one can achieve their dreams by watching, waiting, and wishing but rather by wanting, doing, and pursuing.

What do you want? Seek it! Why do you want it? Go for it! What sacrifices are you willing to make to achieve it? The best way to multiply your efforts as a preacher, teacher, lecturer, and/or speaker is to record your productions and repurpose them into books, devotionals, home studies, or curricula. In order to multiply your efforts as a product producer, you must seek various systems so you don't hold up the process of helping others because your time is short and your pace is slow. Instead, find and build a team of stakeholders who are interested in investing in you, your product, and/or service. Create a process that helps you reduce your effort so you can multiply your impact to influence the masses.

You are not someone's tool to be used and misused. You are not someone's object to be objectified based on their feelings. You are not just a cog in the wheel. You are a living, breathing, walking, talking, moving miracle made in the image of God to be the Master's piece to make change possible here on Earth. Your ability to affect your own life and the world around you is limitless. Whether that effect is positive or negative depends on you. Believing in yourself is the foundation of your success, which comes from knowing who you are. Learn to recognize the truth or absence of it in yourself and others. You must stand in the truth in knowing that you have to be purposeful, powerful and profitable—with or without a homie, lover, friend, spouse, sponsor, and/or accountability partner. How you do anything helps you manifest greater things.

You are the CEO of your destiny, and you are worthy of

living the life you deserve and desire. As you continually remind yourself of your worthiness, you will diminish the imposter syndrome that hijacks the voice of reason that keeps you from your possibilities. In its place, your spirit will echo the Divine's Word that is meant to fuel your soul. Its energy comes from the greatness that is buried deep within you. If you don't know who you are, love who you are, or appreciate who you are, you'll miss out on becoming the fullness of who you are. If you find yourself struggling with accepting that you can live the life you choose to live, you will never live it. If you are continually looking outside of yourself for permission to do what God has commissioned, you won't. Or if you are struggling with the idea that you are more than enough to manifest your hopes and dreams, you won't manifest the miracles within you. When you get a glimpse of a better reflection, or consider whispers of hope, don't allow fear to deafen your ears. Instead, allow truth to make you free.

Unfortunately, when your truth is no longer your truth but attached to the acceptance of others, your truth changes based on your audience. Find your truth by going back to the time you started believing you were no longer completely useless. Protect your truth so you can free yourself to be yourself. Embrace your truth so you evolve into the fullness of who you are, and don't allow your truth to be perverted by your circumstances. You're meant to be more in your life, more in your spirit, more in your walk, and more in your talk. You're not supposed to just be okay with mediocrity and complacency. You're not supposed to be okay with replacing your parents. God has a calling, purpose, expectation that you will choose to manifest pieces of heaven on Earth. You're assigned for someone; you are someone's prayer. You're someone's answer. Yes, you are. You're someone's problem solver—a solution to problems. You are supposed to rise up. You are supposed to boss up. You are supposed to defy your realities. You are supposed to create wealth. You are supposed to be the first millionairess in your family. You are supposed to dominate in your lane and master your zone of genius.

To maximize your potential, you must never forget that God said that He is your present help. He is your way maker. He wants to walk through you. He wants to talk to you. He wants to dream through you. He wants you to become a vessel that he can use. So, you're going to have to get out of your emotions. You're going to have to eject the pain. You must remove the energy and the mind blocks that keep you stuck in your situation. Many biblical lessons teach us that God has already given us what we need to dominate in business. You only need to identify and value what's around or within you to produce, monetize, and multiply. If you're not known for anything, get known for something. Once you have taken all the steps to identify what to name and claim, then you produce it. Whether you're preaching God's word, speaking on stages, offering legal solutions, doing hair, helping others overcome grief, or offering homecare solutions so that senior citizens live comfortably in their own homes, you must continually be fruitful and multiply.

You must hold yourself accountable to have, do, and be who God says you are. You must learn when to ask for help and have the courage to try new things on your own. Believe me when I say, untethering yourself to things and people who hold you to live your best life unapologetically and authentically is the key to manifesting pieces of heaven here on earth. You must overcome the obstacles of traditions. You must overcome the obstacles of racism. God has preordained you to let your light shine, to live your best life, to be fruitful and multiply, and to dominate in every aspect of your life. God has given you enough love, power, and might to manifest an amazing life here on earth. You can turn a pitiful story into a powerful one just by changing your thoughts. You can turn your anger into activated activity by aspiring for greater things. You can change your world by changing your words. You don't have to fear being alone because you never are. You don't have to doubt your path because you have been preordained to prosper. You don't have to stay stuck in your reality because your steps have been ordered by the Most-High God. Nor do you have to live in a story that no longer serves you. You get to choose who you will be. You get to choose your worth. You get to choose how you show up in this world. Free will is your birthright! You get to choose whether you will manifest success on this side of heaven.

About the Author

Through the power of law and speaking, Toni Moore, Esquire has created an unparalleled connection with people around the world. Toni Moore Esquire is a bestselling author, motivational speaker, and Start Up Intellectual Property Attorney who believes our brilliance is our No. 1 wealth-building asset. With over 20+ years in the areas of business development, intellectual property protection, and estate planning, Toni has become known for her "keeping it bossy" mantra that is geared to help women and men alike to live and love their best lives on this side of heaven.

From her traumatized childhood to becoming a triumphant god-girl, Toni navigated blindly in an effort to live the life she dreamed and desired. After graduating from the University of

TONI MOORE ESQ.

Pennsylvania and later the Temple University School of Law, Toni became a sought-after speaker and attorney who always showed up ready to speak and protect the rights of those she served. In addition, Toni is the founder and CEO of The Moore Legal Firm, which serves start-ups and established business owners in the areas of business formation, asset protection, and regulatory compliance.

In addition to lawyering, Toni has secured teaching opportunities with Temple and Eastern University. She has also shared platforms as a speaker with award-winning and bestselling authors and coaches, such as Lisa Nichols, Iyanla Vanzant, Tianna Von Johnson, Jamal Bryant, Willie Jolly, Cheryl Wood, Trevor Otts, and Simon Bailey, just to name a few. In addition, Toni has contributed her pen to the literary industry by authoring four books and co-authoring in over ten book anthologies. To learn more about upleveling your success in life and business, please visit http://mstonimoore.com/.